Building Continuing Bonds for Grieving and Bereaved Children

by the same author

Dream Time with Children
Learning to Dream, Dreaming to Learn
ISBN 978 1 84310 014 0
eISBN 978 1 84642 314 7

Helping Children to Manage Loss
Positive Strategies for Renewal and Growth
ISBN 978 1 85302 605 8
eISBN 978 0 85700 092 7

of related interest

Bereaved Parents and their Continuing Bonds
Love after Death
Catherine Seigal
ISBN 978 1 78592 326 5
eISBN 978 1 78450 641 4

Rafi's Red Racing Car
Explaining Suicide and Grief to Young Children
Louise Moir
ISBN 978 1 78592 200 8
eISBN 978 1 78450 476 2

Remembering Lucy
A Story about Loss and Grief in a School
Sarah Helton
Illustrated by Anna Novy
ISBN 978 1 78592 307 4
eISBN 978 1 78450 614 8

Supporting People through Loss and Grief
An Introduction for Counsellors and Other Caring Practitioners
John Wilson
ISBN 978 1 84905 376 1
eISBN 978 0 85700 739 1

BUILDING CONTINUING BONDS for GRIEVING and BEREAVED CHILDREN

A Guide for Counsellors and Practitioners

BRENDA MALLON

Jessica Kingsley *Publishers*
London and Philadelphia

Permission has been granted for all the case study material from children.

First published in 2018
by Jessica Kingsley Publishers
73 Collier Street
London N1 9BE, UK
and
400 Market Street, Suite 400
Philadelphia, PA 19106, USA

www.jkp.com

Copyright © Brenda Mallon 2018

Front cover image source: Shutterstock®.

Library of Congress Cataloging in Publication Data
A CIP catalog record for this book is available from the Library of Congress

British Library Cataloguing in Publication Data
A CIP catalogue record for this book is available from the British Library

ISBN 978 1 78592 193 3
eISBN 978 1 78450 465 6

Printed and bound in Great Britain

MIX
Paper from
responsible sources
FSC
www.fsc.org   FSC® C013056

Contents

Introduction.   7

1. Keeping Love in Your Heart. 11

2. Harvesting Stories 27

3. Keeping Up Conversations 39

4. Guiding Lights: Dreams and Spirituality 61

5. Loving Yourself when Someone You Love Has Died . . 77

6. Making Memories Together when Someone You Love
   Is Dying 93

7. Useful Resources 111

   References 129

   Subject Index 139

   Author Index 143

INTRODUCTION

The charity Childhood Bereavement UK estimates that over 100 children and young people are bereaved of a parent each day (CBN 2016). More are bereaved of a sibling, grandparent, friend or neighbour. This means that one in 29 children and young people in the UK have been bereaved of a parent or sibling, which is the equivalent of one child in every classroom. Every day someone dies, including those who die unexpectedly. In 2016, 525,048 people died in England and Wales (ONS 2016). That leaves a lot of bereaved people who have to adjust to a world that has completely changed for them (Harrison 2002).

The death of someone close has a profound psychological impact on each of us. As adults we have greater life experiences and a more mature awareness of death; however, children and young people, with less experience of death and anticipatory loss, find that bereavement, as a new experience, can be frightening, shocking and bewildering. According to Colin Murray Parkes, a consultant psychiatrist, we live in an 'assumptive world' (Parkes 1988) – we assume that our routine and daily life will carry on as it has always done, but that world can be shattered at any moment, as traumatic events demonstrate. It can destabilise the world we know and transform our lives.

Children assume, as we all do, that our everyday life will continue with its familiar routines. However, when their world is turned upside down by a bereavement, their lives are irrevocably changed and will never be the same again. Their feeling of security is compromised and they may feel they have no control in their life, which undermines their confidence. The transition children and young people make after experiencing a death is the 'work' of mourning; they then need the support of adults to move through a territory that has no map as they learn to make meaning of what has happened to them (Neimeyer 2012).

Bereavement in childhood brings changes and challenges. As children grow, a bereaved young person may feel different from his peers,[1] feel inadequate, guilt, isolated and confused. This can detract from his natural resilience and lead to under-achievement at school, if not exclusion. This also impacts on the young person's ability to build and maintain social relationships – it is hard to be a friend when you feel so useless and insignificant. For those readers who need an educational perspective, I have written extensively on how school staff can support children (see Mallon 1998, 2011), and refer them to these works.

The process of grieving is not about detaching from the dead person, or deliberately seeking to forget about them. Nor is it about passing through stages of grief until gaining 'closure'. Rather, it is about remembering and changing our attachment to the dead person. We do not forget and our relationship does not end at death. The process of grieving has to include remembering: recalling images and revisiting events that took place. This is a painful process and, in a sense, grieving never ends, but the initial extreme pain does pass, and we move to a place of memories rather than being with a raw wound. In order to help bereaved and grieving children we can show them how continued connections to the dead might sustain and enrich their lives as they grieve, grow and mature.

---

1   I have used 'his/he' and 'her/she' in alternating chapters in this book.

Grieving is a process, not a single act. Children often re-visit their loss as they reach different milestones, such as when they transfer to a different school or college, and as they reach anniversaries or special celebrations such as Christmas or Eid. Grieving takes as long as it takes. We have continuing bonds with those who have died, and these bonds may be crucial in sustaining us through the pain of loss.

We will explore these continuing bonds throughout this book. While loss may be an intensely difficult time for a child, it may also bring about personal growth and increased self-awareness. Children may not only survive, but also thrive. They may develop increased resilience and have enhanced skills in dealing with future adversity (Monroe and Oliviere 2007). We consider this in greater depth in Chapter 2.

All quotes from children, unless otherwise stated, are from my work with children.

LOOKING AFTER YOURSELF

There are simple things that you can do that value the child and help him through a time of enormous impact and, while doing that, cherish yourself. It is important to recognise that your own experiences of loss may be re-awakened, and to understand that at times you will feel inadequate or hopeless; but remember, you're not a magician who can make things better with the flick of a wand. You are a human being who can be there to offer whatever you can of your own positive self. Always seek support from colleagues if you are unsure about what to do or if you feel overwhelmed. Remember the proverb, 'we cannot direct the wind, but we can adjust the sails.'

Anyone in a caring role needs time for reflection and time to think about how to replace depleted energy. Creativity, making art, making space in your life for joy and making your life meaningful, these all bring the opportunity to top up your resources when you are giving so much to others in need. Taking good care of yourself is vitally important – don't stint on this.

There is an African proverb that says, 'It takes a whole village to raise a child.' Accepting its wisdom, we can ask others to help with grieving children. Whether a parent, friend, teacher or neighbour, you can all be part of the healing process, and just as you seek support for children, seek it for yourself when you need it.

Chapter 1

KEEPING LOVE IN YOUR HEART

Unlike adults, children move in and out of grief. One minute they are inconsolable and ten minutes later they are asking if they can play with a friend. Like clouds that scurry over the sun, the light and shade can change moment by moment. As those who care for children, it is worth remembering that this is nature's way of protecting them from the intensity of their experience. As François de La Rochefoucauld, a noted French author, stated, 'Neither the sun nor death can be looked at without winking.'[1] Children pick up their grief then put it down again, like jumping in and out of puddles (Crossley 2000). What sustains children in the grieving process is the love that surrounds them:

> The child's experience of grief is very different [from that in adults] and can best be described as intermittent and profound involvement in the thoughts and emotions related to and generated by the loss. These pockets of grief are wholly absorbing at the time, ones which remove the child from the here and now and immerse him in grief. The experience finishes as quickly as it comes, leaving the child to re-orientate himself back into what is happening around him.

---

1 See http://bestlifequotesblog.com/insightful-maxims-francois-de-la-rochefoucauld

(Peta Hemmings, senior practitioner, Barnardo's Orchard Project, quoted in Smith and Pennells 1995)

'*The dual model of coping with loss*', introduced by Margaret Stroebe and Henk Schut (1999), demonstrates how the bereaved move between loss-oriented behaviour and restoration-oriented behaviour. Loss-oriented behaviour includes grief work, mourning, the intrusion of sadness and an inability to escape from thoughts about the deceased. Restoration-oriented behaviour includes attending to changes in everyday life, doing new things, finding distractions from grief, new roles, identity and new relationships. The bereaved child often oscillates between these like a pendulum swinging between opposite points.

Through the process of grieving the child invests in her future while still having a bond with the loved one who has died. Children who are bereaved have the right to remember the person who has died for the rest of their lives, if they want to do so. These memories may include both positive and negative memories, the good ones and the difficult ones, and the deceased person becomes a part of the child's continuing life story.

THE VALUE OF CONTINUING BONDS

Phyllis Silverman, noted researcher, teacher and author, and J. William Worden, a founding member of the Association of Death Education and Counseling (ADEC) and a pioneer in the hospice movement in the US, carried out seminal research into children's experience of bereavement (Silverman and Worden 1992). One intrinsic part of the grieving process, they discovered, is the establishment of a set of memories, feelings and actions, which they refer to as 'constructing the deceased'. This helps build an ongoing link with the deceased while recognising that the person is dead and will not be physically present in the child's life again.

The process, Silverman stated, involved five stages that reflected the child's efforts to maintain the connection to the deceased parent. First was locating the deceased, usually 'in heaven'; second, experiencing the deceased, for instance, believing the deceased is watching the child; third, reaching out to the deceased in thoughts; fourth, waking memories; and fifth, cherishing linking objects. These continuing bonds provide an emotional anchor for the young person as they sail in the unmapped seas of bereavement. In working with bereaved children we can help foster these connections, these continuing bonds. As Frank Brennan and Michael Dash say, 'Bereavement affects the continuing life of the grieving mourner; there is no need to let go or get over it' (Brennan and Dash 2009, p.35).

Silverman and her fellow researchers concluded that bereavement 'should not be viewed as a psychological state that ends or from which one recovers; rather, it should be understood as a cognitive and emotional process that occurs in a social context of which the deceased is part' (Silverman and Worden 1992, p.497; Silverman 2000). The social context is the family, the neighbourhood and the wider community to which the dead person belonged and is remembered by.

Craig Vickio's research (1999) into the adaptive value of continuing bonds focused on five strategies for connecting with the deceased. The first is recognising how the deceased has left an imprint on our lives; second, deriving a sense of meaning from the life of the deceased; and third, using objects that symbolically link us to the deceased. Fourth is identifying ceremonial opportunities to include the deceased in our lives; and finally, we continue our connection in reviewing the deceased's life story.

Expressions of continuing bonds, such as dreaming of the deceased, keeping possessions or photographs, or feeling their presence, are common across cultures (Foster *et al.* 2012), although they are influenced by local religious and cultural practices. In the Taoist Chinese tradition, for example, priests will advise the bereaved family that the spirits of the deceased will visit from time to time, and especially seven days after the death took place (Chan *et al.* 2005).

A study in Ecuador (Foster *et al.* 2012) found that 98 per cent of the participants, including adults and children, purposely chose reminders of the deceased and 47 per cent reported reminiscing about the deceased person as a way of staying connected. Twenty-nine per cent communicated with the deceased as a way to remember and connect. Some spoke to their loved one while others chose writing as a form of communication. An eleven-year-old boy communicated with his father through writing letters and leaving them at the cemetery. He said, 'I write to him and say that I won't forget him at all' (quoted in Foster *et al.* 2012, p.124).

In her research into continuing bonds after bereavement in Japanese and British culture, researcher Christine Valentine found that connection with the deceased is an important aspect of both cultures. Present-day Japanese people, while still continuing ancestral practices (such as erecting a shrine in the home and placing offerings of flowers and food there), are becoming more influenced by Western practices, instigating more individual and personalised forms of continued connection. British people 'spoke of bonds with the deceased that reflected interdependency, a concern with the well-being of the deceased loved ones and a desire to integrate them into the lives of the living' (Valentine 2009, p.11).

Narrative therapy, developed by Michael White in Australia (a former social worker and family therapist), affirms the ongoing relationship with the dead rather than dwelling on the finality of death. It helps people to find inner resources and strengths they can use in the transition time when their loved one is dying and after death. It concentrates on what has been gained by the mourner's relationship with the deceased rather than what has been lost, and considers how to include the dead in the mourner's continuing life. It also promotes the remembering of relationships and lives that have been shared (Hedtke 2000). Children may remember more than we think, particularly where they are with people who were with them during the event or in a situation that prompts memories to surface (Gopnik, Meltzoff and Kuhl 1999).

In narrative therapy the story is seen as the basic unit of experience. Stories guide how people act, feel, think and make sense of new experiences. It focuses on how these stories get written and re-written. Each day we unconsciously update our life stories in response to new events in our lives. For children and young people this can be a demanding task as they grow and develop, but when something like the death of someone close to them happens, the story may be at crisis point, and they need others to help them make sense of it. Just as with the work of White discussed above, the making and gathering of a life story aid people to make meaning of their experiences.

Those left behind by death can continue a relationship with the deceased after the sadness, anger, guilt, relief or whatever the emotional responses, have passed. As Robert Anderson, the playwright, said, after the death of his first wife, 'Death ends a life, but it does not end a relationship, which struggles on in the survivor's mind toward some resolution which it never finds' (Anderson 1974, p.77). How do we help children to find and accept what they have been given so that they can keep those legacies in their hearts forever? How do we foster continuing bonds? We need to actively help the child, because, as Julie Stokes, founder of Winston's Wish (a leading charity that offers support to children who have been bereaved by the loss of a parent or sibling) says, 'memories don't sit there like a stone. They have to be worked like the best bread, kneaded and gently warmed so [they] can slowly rise to the surface' (Stokes 2004).

A boy I counselled many years ago was bereaved when his father died suddenly in a sporting accident. We read Susan Varley's book *Badger's Parting Gifts* (2013) together. In the story, the old Badger, knowing he will die soon and realising his friends will be sad, creates a legacy for each of his forest friends. He taught Frog to skate on ice, he showed Fox how to knot a tie and he gave Mrs Rabbit his special gingerbread recipe. Each of the many animals had a special memory of what Badger had taught them to do, and every time they did the thing, they remembered their loving friend. These parting gifts continue the bonds they shared with Badger. I asked the boy if his father had left him any legacies. He told me that his dad had taught him to whistle. He whistled a tune and was proud that he could do it. It will be a life-long connection to his father.

What about the term 'closure' in relation to bereavement? Closure implies that the link with the dead will be ended, which can be confusing and counter-intuitive for adults as well as for children. Love is not like water flowing through a tap that can be shut off and held back. Rather, the continuing bonds of love may never be broken or cease. They will always be part of the child's story and part of the child's history. There is an imperative about 'closure' that can make people feel ill at ease because they have not reached this mythical state.

SPECIAL DAYS

Children don't 'get over' the death of someone they love; instead they spend the rest of their lives accommodating the absence of the person they loved and keeping that love in their heart. In the first year, special days such as birthdays, Father's Day, Mother's Day, festive and significant religious events may be difficult to face as feelings of loss are exacerbated. However, such feelings continue in the second year when fewer people remember the child's loss. Important life events, those significant milestones, will remind the young person and the adults they become of the absence of that person in their life: 'At each new milestone, the loss of someone whom we care for deeply is redefined and grief is revisited' (Schonfeld and Demaria 2016, e8).

Anniversaries can act as grief triggers as children revisit loss; but other triggers may also occur, such as if a child smells the same perfume her mother wore or hears a song that her grandfather used to sing. The events may come out of the blue and are difficult to anticipate; like a huge wave breaking on the shore, they can knock you sideways and bring you to your knees.

Matt and Joanna's twin sons died at one month and one week old. The first Christmas after their death was particularly hard. Matt said, 'We always set aside some special time for our boys at Christmas...over the years this has manifested into a much happier time where we chat to them and toast them with a glass of champagne. They even both have their own stocking by the fire place' (CBUK 2017c).

Marking special days can be an important aspect of a bereaved child's life. Spending time with friends and family who were close to the person who died can reinforce connection. Where the child has few memories of the time before death, collecting thoughts and memories from these friends and family can add to their knowledge and reinforce the presence in their lives.

Over my years working with bereaved children and their families, I have found the following activities helpful on anniversaries where grief 'aftershocks' may occur:

- Going to a special place that was important to the child and to the person who died.

- Taking flowers to the special place.

- Writing a letter to tell the person what is good in the child's life.

- Listening to favourite music or music the loved person liked.

- Planning a special event or ritual for the anniversary, one that is personal to the child or special to the child's religious or cultural tradition.

- Tying a message to a balloon and letting it float up into the sky.

- Lighting a candle to mark the special day.

- Being with others who can share memories and retell stories of the deceased person's life.

- Children reminding themselves what they loved about the person and the gifts or legacies they left.

The mother of one little boy whose father had died – the one who asked me if I wanted to hear him whistle – arranged a small memory table on the anniversary of his father's death.

Her two sons, their grandparents and firm family friends were invited to put objects and messages on the table. They celebrated their fond memories of him and the joy they shared when he was alive.

RESILIENCE

The term 'resilience' comes from material science and denotes the property of being able to recover from stress without lasting damage (Wilson, Gabriel and James 2016). Some describe it as being like a rubber band – at its full potential it is stretched, yet flexible, and it can spring back. For bereaved children, resilience is the ability to manage the loss and to invest in a life where the deceased is not present. Resilience is partly based on temperament and personality, and partly on support networks offered by friends, family and others in the community. As one bereaved young person said, 'I had a good strong family, we all pulled together and grieved as a family, but I feel for young people and children who might not have this and will need help in other ways' (CBN no date).

A resilient child is not only a child in a certain set of circumstances, but ultimately a child with a certain set of attitudes (Brooks and Goldstein 2001). We can help children by enabling them to develop stress hardiness. These are coping competencies that include self-understanding, managing emotions and developing social skills so that children are more able to manage the adverse situations that life brings their way. In building stress hardiness so that children develop a resilient mindset, we can enable them to handle the stress of grief more effectively. We can aid this process by providing consistency, care and continuity.

We may need to coach children to help them develop a more resilient mindset. Focusing on positive memories may help, such as thinking about special times the child had with the deceased, something they laughed at together, a memory that offers comfort, something the child liked about the dead person and something the child valued about the relationship (Stokes 2004). Physical activity that is adventurous and challenging can also be helpful in building resilience, especially with boys, who may hide their grief behind a mask of tough stoicism (Pollack 2006).

Winston's Wish has carried out extensive research into how children respond to bereavement. They concluded that children bereaved of a parent:

> generally experience a better outcome when they have a secure attachment and positive relationship with at least one competent adult (ideally their surviving parent if they have one); maintain a healthy connection to the dead person; engage well with their peers and have an area of competence that they and society value. (Stokes 2009, p.10)

So what is a resilient mindset? A central factor is the possession of hope in the future and the capacity to trust others and to risk building secure attachments. Crucially important is the capacity to talk about the dead person in a way that brings comfort and warmth and maintains a positive bond. We can aid children by helping them to find meaning in their life and their future. The child's family, friends, teachers and neighbours can all play a part in building these positive aspects that will build resilience, as can specialist child bereavement services (Stubbs *et al.* 2008). Also, the faith community of the child and wider social groups such as scouts, sports clubs and leisure activities with others, all have a part to play in helping the child to value herself and to recognise her place in the wider world.

Stress-resistant people have the following characteristics:

- an ability to welcome change and embrace it as a normal part of life

- a sense of commitment

- ability to take responsibility for oneself

- optimistic outlook

- capacity to persevere

- capacity to perform under pressure

- courage

- humour.

To build resilience in young people:

- listen to what they say

- hear what they say

- spend time with them and really focus on them

- share something with them – thoughts, ideas, feelings

- cultivate the capacity to survive in adversity

- cultivate the capacity to thrive in adversity

- cultivate the capacity to achieve despite adversity

- laugh with them whenever there is an opportunity

- help them to see the positive side of life

- encourage them to try new things

- cultivate gratitude even for the smallest things

- trust their inner wisdom – we have so much to learn from them

- focus on their best qualities, and nourish them as you would a blossoming young plant.

When a young person's life has been unexpectedly altered and she manages to adapt to that change, it can build up confidence and courage to face changes that inevitably happen in all our lives. As Adam Golightly writes in his *Guardian* column 'Widower of the Parish', 'Bereavement is dreadful, but once you accept that the life you had is unrecoverable, you might just be able to create a new one that isn't simply the old version but sadder' (2016).

Resilience may also be fostered by enabling the child to look towards their future: What would they like to do in the future? What would they like to achieve? What work would make them happy? What strengths do they feel they have and what could they do to develop them? By naming examples of resilience young people can identify in their own lives and in the lives of other people they admire, we can help them to map their own personal resilience. Also, by helping young people to make realistic plans about how they may frame their future, we enable them to see that they *have* a future despite the loss they have experienced.

CARING FOR MEMORIES

Harvard anthropologist Arthur Kleinman, in his article 'Caring for memories', says, 'Care giving does not end with the loss of the person cared for. We go on caring for memories. Memories moreover, can and do become so vivid, we literally re-member the dead person. So that he or she continues to be a presence among us' (Kleinman 2016, p.56). Both individuals and societies find ways to keep the memory of the dead present in everyday life. We establish cultural myths, erect memorial monuments, statues and plaques, and establish social rituals such as Remembrance Day in the UK that celebrates the sacrifice of soldiers in war. In these ways their memories live on and our connections with them are reinforced.

The memorial may take various forms according to the culture in which the deceased lived. It might be influenced by ethnic aspects as well as by historical or geographical traditions. As Tony Walter, Reader in Sociology, states, 'funeral celebrants have to produce a story that works for not just them but also for friends, colleagues and neighbours' (Walter 2006, p.25).

Roadside memorials and spontaneous shrines make grief visible and are found increasingly throughout the world (MacConville 2010). We see them at the place where an accident has caused a death, for example, when a cyclist has been killed. They reflect the love that the bereaved feel for their loved one. Sometimes a white-painted bicycle, a 'ghost bike', may be placed there to mark the spot where the death happened and to act as a warning to others to take care. They also act as a form of remembrance and continued connection to the dead person.

For some families and children the site of the death and the memorial site becomes the place of continuing dialogue with the dead. Flowers, relevant objects such as teddy bears where a child has died, or school ties and photographs where a school friend has died, are often placed at the site.

When the football player George Best died, the thoroughfare outside Manchester United's ground was covered in scarves, flowers, United strip football kit and candles. Messages in cards, on copies of newspapers featuring Best in his prime and on t-shirts reflected the loss and anguish of his fans. This public 'memorialisation' indicates the continuing bonds – 'We'll never forget you George', 'Always in our hearts' – and, in 2015, fans brought a new tribute ten years after his death, in the form of a banner with the words 'Georgie... Simply the Best'. It hangs in the stadium as a memorial to a much-loved player. Children who were supporters of Manchester United when George Best died were adults in 2015 when the banner was installed. Their continuing bonds were affirmed in both the visual memorial and in the ritual singing that celebrated his life. Such public figures demonstrate how continuing bonds are part of our common humanity: families and friends die just as those in the public eye die.

For many family members bereaved by death in a public space, the place of death is where they feel closest to the deceased. I recall a woman speaking on an Australian radio programme, in which she said, 'It's where he lost his life and where he will always be... I won't go out to the cemetery because that's not where he is...he is here at the cross.' Such sites can also be a place of pilgrimage where family and friends feel a sense of closeness and continuing connection.

MEMENTOS HAVE MEANING

When we are with bereaved children, part of our role is to help them recall positive memories that allow continuing bonds to develop. Mementos are there to say, 'We existed together... This is not just my imagination... My belief in being loved (i.e. by a lost loved one) is validated' (Di Ciacco 2008, p.83).

Tangible objects, images in photographs, videos of family times together and audiotapes with the voice of the loved person all help to make their time together a real, concrete part of their lives.

The Foundling Museum in London explores the history of the Foundling Hospital, the first UK children's charity, and first public art gallery. It was set up in 1739 by the philanthropist Thomas Coram to care for babies at risk of being abandoned by their destitute mothers. There is a collection of poignant mementos, or 'tokens', as they are known, from desperate mothers who gave their babies up into the care of the hospital. They include everyday objects, buttons, ribbons, pictures and punctured or engraved pennies with a special mark. The hope for these women was that one day they would return to claim their child and would be able to tell the authorities what the identifying token for their child was.

In his project, 'Superman was a Foundling', for the Foundling Museum, poet Lemn Sissay, MBE, explored the powerful role orphaned, fostered and adopted children have in our culture's literature and films (Sissay 2014). These are also part of 'The hero's journey', the stories and scripts of our own lives based on the idea of 'The hero's journey', and how this often mirrors the lives of grieving children. We explore this in more depth in Chapter 2.

It was common in the Victorian era to take photographs of the dead, particularly children, to be kept by the living. These images are often staged so that the dead person is propped up in a tableau with other family members. Their eyes were often painted open to increase their natural, life-like appearance. In the novel for young adults, *The Lie Tree*, the protagonist thinks about her dead brothers and mementos attached to them. 'No such photographs had been taken of Faith's little departed brothers. They were remembered through other mementos, their baby bottles carefully preserved or their hair sewn into samplers' (Hardinge 2015, p.90).

MEMORY BOXES

Memory boxes can be an important possession for bereaved children. In a specially decorated box children can collect objects that were significant to the person who has died. Bereaved children I have worked with have included a photograph, a video, a letter and a mobile phone. They have also included perfume or a favourite soap that link to the smell they associated with the parent who died. Some children kept an article of clothing. These 'linking objects' carry profound meaning for children that they can keep throughout their life and that they can reopen and reminisce about when they choose to do so.

In *How to Look for a Lost Dog* (2016), the novelist Ann Martin reveals how a box left by her mother affects 11-year-old Rose:

> On a shelf in the coat closet is a box, a hatbox. The top and bottom are held together by a white satin braid. The braid is fraying, which leads me to believe that the box and the braid are old. Also, the box used to be blue, but over the years the blue has faded to a lighter and lighter shade. Now it's pale grey.
>
> Inside the box are things that belonged to my mother, before she left… I wish my mother had written something on the box, something like *These things are important to me* or *Gifts for Rose* or even just *Treasures*. But there are no words or clues of any sort. (Martin 2016, p.64)

In the box is 'the necklace that has a silver bird's nest hanging from it. Inside the nest are three pearls (purls) that are fake and are supposed to be birds' eggs. What does the necklace say about my mother?' (p.65). Then there is a seashell, a photo of a black cat, a pin with a little silver badge in the shape of 'R' for 'Rose', Rose's parents' wedding announcement, Rose's hospital bracelet, and a scarf with a picture of a rose on it.

For Rose these objects feel like a tangible connection to her missing mother. In creating memory boxes children and young people have control about what they choose to keep.

They may also include drawings or letters to their parent and any they have received from them.

MAKING A MEMORY JOURNAL

A child's life is like a piece of paper on which every passerby leaves a mark.

Chinese proverb

Children fear losing the memory of the person who has died. They can be helped to remember by making their own memory journal. This is particularly the case for younger children who become distressed when they cannot remember Mummy's face or the way she looked. Photographs taken with the parent or sibling and pasted into a journal can act as an ongoing connection to the person and be a perpetual memento to comfort the child (Gordon 1995).

Making a journal can be a powerful experience for a bereaved child. It can include writing, pictures and photographs; in fact, anything that allows the child to recall the deceased loved one. In writing, the child can recall times spent together as well as their relationship. In helping a child make a memory journal you may find the following prompts may make it easier for the child or young person to focus. They can complete these as sentences and take as much space and time as they want to – there are no hard and fast rules:

- What was important in your relationship with your special person?
- Physical description and special characteristics.
- My special memory.
- Story/history of the person, which you know about.
- Special time you had together.
- Favourite foods.
- Favourite things you liked to do.

- Friends or relatives who were important.

- Funny incidents you remember.

- A letter to your special person on their birthday.

- What did you learn from your special person?

This activity could be followed by making a collage with photographs or magazine cut-outs that reflect the hobbies and joys of the person, or perhaps pictures of food the person liked to eat.

As we help children and young people to keep love in their hearts, we enable them to discover their own capacity to love others too.

Chapter 2

HARVESTING STORIES

The well-known nursery rhyme, 'Humpty Dumpty', is a story in poetic form:

> Humpty Dumpty sat on a wall.
> Humpty Dumpty had a great fall.
> All the king's horses and all the king's men
> Couldn't put Humpty Dumpty together again.

Bereavement is a 'Humpty Dumpty' situation. Nothing can be done about it. The one thing that most people want cannot happen – the dead cannot be brought back to life, just as Humpty Dumpty couldn't be put back together again. In our work with children we are there as fellow human beings. A child who is bereaved is another human being whose emotions impact on his daily life. Just as the school staff, doctors, nurses and care workers bring their feelings over the work threshold, children bring their feelings into the everyday situations they encounter. You don't have to be a therapist to help; you just have to be a caring, humane, human being. We share a common humanity: to live is to feel pain, and to love is to grieve. Grief is the price we pay for love.

As human beings we share physical characteristics: we are all born, we grow and we learn. We share emotions such as joy, love, fear and sadness. While we clearly have different life experiences, we still have the basic needs that Maslow describes in his 'hierarchy of needs' (Maslow 1943). It is this shared nature of being human that enables all of us to help a grieving child, to be part of the healing process. And in that healing process the stories that we listen to and share are crucially important.

In the introduction to his book *Counting Stars*, award-winning children's author David Almond says, 'Like all stories, they merge memory and dream, the real and the imagined, truth and lies. And, perhaps like all stories, they are an attempt to re-assemble what is fragmented, to rediscover what has been lost... I think stories are living things – among the most important things in the world' (2000, p.ix). This series of stories about his childhood are pertinent to the way we work with children. If we encourage children to tell the stories that are important to them, to keep the bonds with their own past and to the people who were important to them, living or dead, we facilitate their mourning:

> Stories, however wonderful, however universal their appeal, will simply die unless they are told. Each storyteller must re-interpret them for a new audience to enjoy. Grandparents do the same thing with family stories... Without [these stories], as without the ancient tales of old, we are left stranded both intellectually and emotionally. (Morpurgo 2006)

Thus, for Michael Morpurgo, the grandparent and the storyteller, stories provide the next generation with an emotional and cultural link through which values, beliefs and experiences are passed on and given new life. The individual person and the individual story are shown to be valuable, not merely for their own sake, but as part of a broader spectrum of interconnectedness. We build continuing bonds that enhance our sense of continuity in what can feel as a highly unstable world. The anchor to the past brings a sense of security.

Bereaved children have the right to tell their story in a variety of ways and as often as they need to. As adults we need to listen in whatever way they choose to tell it – in words, drawings, acting or letters. We should encourage whatever medium is preferred by the child. Stephen Grosz, psychoanalyst and psychotherapist, wrote the wonderful book, *The Examined Life*, based on his work with clients of all ages. He said, 'I'm a great believer that anything, no matter how complicated and theoretical, that can be done in technical language, can be done better in a very simple story... We are all storytellers – we make stories to make sense of our lives. But it is not enough to tell tales. There must be someone to listen' (quoted in Round 2013).

Stories of past events, of sustenance and hope, even in situations that seem desperate, can help children and young people feel enriched and empowered. We create stories about our lives as a way of understanding the life we have lived and are living, to find a sense of order and meaning. Life is full of uncertainty and ambiguity, and in making stories we are trying to make sense of these feelings (Carey 2005).

We carry the deceased with us since they are part of our lives, and we carry them with us in the stories we recall and retell about them (Walter 1999). We adjust to life without their physical presence and accommodate them in our hearts and minds. According to Oliver Jeffers, a Northern Irish artist, illustrator and writer, 'We are after all, little more than the stories we are told, the stories we tell, and those that are told about us' (2016, p.4).

THE HERO'S JOURNEY

The hero's journey has an archetypal story pattern that is found in folk tales, fairy stories, myths and legends, as well as present-day adventures. They bring us the experience of thousands of years of dealing with situations that threaten survival, as described by American mythological researcher Joseph Campbell in *The Hero with a Thousand Faces* (1993). In the hero's journey the heroine or hero kills the monster, takes brave actions and survives to overcome the dangers that beset them (Turner 2001).

The typical structure in a hero's journey begins with separation, departure from his familiar world, initiation where the hero has to learn to find a way through in an unfamiliar world then, after finding friends, overcoming those who would harm him, facing adversity and coming through it only to return to his earlier familiar world with a new understanding of himself and his world, and to have grown in strength and spirit. In many ways, the hero's journey is the journey of the bereaved child or young person.

Charlie Higson, author of the Young Bond book series, commented that his hero, like all children in adventure books, has to be an orphan. Batman was orphaned when he first appeared in DC comics in 1939, but long before that, in 1697, after the death of her mother, Cinderella fared badly at the hands of her stepmother and two stepsisters, when her father was physically or emotionally absent. However, she overcame her trials to win her prince and her freedom from drudgery. Courage, not strength, is the essence of the hero's journey. Confronting fear is not enjoyable but it has to be done in order to not waste personal energy suppressing feelings that have to be faced.

Dorothy Gale, in *The Wizard of Oz* (Baum 1982), was adopted by her aunt and uncle. She meets the Tin Man, the Scarecrow and the Cowardly Lion, all on journeys that are full of adversity but which they overcome to gain the gifts they so desire. The hero's journey is seen in so many stories – *Game of Thrones, Lord of the Rings, The Lion King* and *Star Wars*, to name but a few. The hero comes back from his journey with the power to give benefits to his community as well as discovering inner strength to sustain him in his life.

Harry Potter is taken into the misnamed 'care' of his aunt and uncle after his parents died, as we find out in *Harry Potter and the Philosopher's Stone* (Rowling 1997). Frodo Baggins, in *Lord of the Rings*, was adopted, as was Mowgli in *The Jungle Book*, Estella in *Great Expectations*, Oliver Twist and Jane Eyre. So many of our heroic characters were orphaned, including Han Solo in 'Star Wars', Jamal Malik in 'Slumdog Millionaire', Oliver Twist and Dick Whittington too. Each character had to overcome the loss in their lives and make their way, emotionally and physically, to find safety and personal fulfilment. Such stories give hope and cultivate resilience.

These stories can help children overcome their own monstrous fears including the fear of death. As psychoanalyst Ira Yalom says, 'Children's concerns about death are pervasive and exert far-reaching influence on their experiential worlds. Death is a great enigma to them, and one of their major developmental tasks is to deal with fears of helplessness and obliteration' (Yalom 1980, p.76).

British comedian Paul Chowdhry's mother died when he was five years old. Speaking of his experience, he said, 'You don't quite understand it when you're five. The only things you see are superheroes who have lost a parent and become a superhero. But that doesn't help a child. When you're five you don't get it – you think they'll come back' (quoted in Saner 2017, p.30). Quite often children do not recognise that superheroes suffer drawbacks, uncertainty and often feel inadequate on their journey. Paul, in reflecting on his road to the happily married man and father he is now, spoke of his difficulties growing up and of people who helped him get back on track. In overcoming his adversity following the death of his mother, he echoes some of the characteristics of the hero's journey.

YOUR HEROIC JOURNEY

If you think back to stories from childhood or films that have left a lasting impression on you, the chances are that they are about someone facing adversity and, through resilience, not only surviving but also thriving.

J.M. Barrie, the creator of Peter Pan, was greatly influenced by the death of his brother. When he was six years old, his older brother, David, died in an ice-skating accident, two days before his 14th birthday. His mother was devastated, and to try and ease her pain, J.M. Barrie wore his brother's clothes and began whistling like David. The family took some comfort from the idea that David would be forever young, and that he would never grow old. This idea so influenced J.M. Barrie that he developed the character of Peter Pan who never grows up. The author turned his grief and loss into literature.

Just as in the hero's journey, J.M. Barrie experienced loss and separation in his early life yet overcame adversity to become a literary giant and was appointed a Baronet. Before he died, he bequeathed the royalties for *Peter Pan* to Great Ormond Street Children's Hospital in London.

Scott Becker and Roger Knudson, in their research into mourning (2003), found that remembering the dead and thinking of the stories of their lives helps in the grieving process. As they say, 'The Dead help us write their stories – ours as well. In a sense every story has a ghost writer...' (2003, p.714).

If you reflect on your own life you may find that you have been on an heroic journey. Writing about your own experiences can be rewarding and therapeutic, as the work of James Pennebaker, an American psychologist, shows. He believes that when we put our traumatic experiences into words, we tend to become less concerned with the emotional events that have been weighing us down (Pennebaker 1997). Also, if you are using the hero's journey with children, it is beneficial to have worked experientially in this way so you have a clearer understanding of the value of the process and what it entails.

YOUR HERO'S JOURNEY SCRIPT

Take some time to reflect on your life so far. Are there elements that you have experienced that fit this journey? Write down your responses to the following in a private journal:

- Separation: what are your early experiences of separation? Were you bereaved in your early years?

- Did you change your location?

- Can you think of any adverse situations that impacted on you and your family?

- Were there any particular people, peers or adults, who made your life difficult?

- Were there any particular people, peers or adults, who were particularly helpful?

- Did you have a task to complete or goals to achieve? Were these self-imposed or did other people give them to you?

- What aspects of your character were most helpful to you as you moved through your life, for example, courage, tenacity, kindness, a talent for happiness?

- What have you learned from adverse situations that might have seemed insurmountable at the time?

- If you had one message to give to your younger self, what would it be?

In completing this piece of reflective writing you will be more in tune with the idea of the hero's journey and may be able to see more the amazing heroic journeys that our children experience.

Mithra Nandoo (quoted in CBUK 2017a) reflected on the death of her mother, which happened when she was 11 years old. At that time no one told her that her mother was very ill and likely to die. When her father told her she did not believe it: 'I was in such denial that I refused to go to the funeral.' It took her five years to cry and to go to her mother's grave. She said, 'I was still angry with both my parents for not being honest with me. I didn't have the chance to say goodbye and I felt cheated.' Now, aged 40, with two children, she understands her parents were trying to protect her, shielding her from pain, but should she be in a similar situation, she would tell her children the truth based on their age and understanding. Her heroic journey brought her through disbelief, denial, anger and acceptance, to wise motherhood.

STORIES OF UNEXPECTED GIFTS

Tragedy and loss can unexpectedly give us gifts (Ribbens McCarthy and Jessop 2005). Jo, whose mother died when she was 14, told me that being with her father and two younger brothers after the death gave her a 'get on with it' attitude. 'I knew I had to help with the boys, to get on with my life and do well at school so I could get a chance of having a good job, that paid well and that allowed me to have the life I wanted.' She added, 'I know that was what my Mum wanted for me too.' So Jo, as she said, 'got her head down, and got on with it.' She is absolutely certain that the death of her mother was a source of her determination, although she did not deny the impact of her loss. It also made her less fearful of change. Sometimes when a parent dies the eldest child in particular may be the glue that holds the remaining family together by continuing rituals that the family shared, such as celebrating birthdays and anniversaries. This was something that Jo spontaneously took up.

There is evidence that for some people, children included, traumatic experiences can lead to post-traumatic growth (PTG). A study conducted by Kayo Hirooka and colleagues in Japan found that social factors such as having fun with friends, visiting the deceased parent's grave and 'putting palms together in front of a parent's picture or an altar' enhanced PTG following parental death by cancer (Hirooka *et al.* 2017). As David Schonfeld and Thomas Demaria point out, 'Children who have experienced traumatic events or significant losses in the context of sufficient support and internal capacity to cope may experience posttraumatic growth and emerge with increased resiliency and new skills to cope with future adversity' (2016, e8).

Andy was 17 when his father died. The experience was devastating and felt like a physical blow, like 'someone's chopped off my leg'; however, the bond with his dead father also gave him strength: '...my dad passing away kind of motivated me more on my college work. Like during my A-levels – it was just a sort of driving force. That's probably why I am here [at university] and it's probably made my dad proud' (quoted in Valentine 2009, p.8). Notice how he speaks of his relationship with his father as being able to know what has happened to his son, as a continuing presence.

In his book *David and Goliath*, Malcolm Gladwell (2013), an English-born Canadian journalist, author and speaker, notes the high number of people in power or at the top of their profession who experienced the death of a parent during childhood. He describes them as 'eminent orphans' who are driven by a search for purpose and meaning in their lives and a need to fill the emptiness caused by the hole in their lives that can never truly be filled but must be accommodated in some way. As Gladwell puts it, 'The act of facing overwhelming odds produces greatness and beauty' (2013, p.6).

For some who experience trauma there is a feeling that, 'if I can survive that, I can survive anything'. They have managed to come through and feel an increased sense of empathy and resilience. Some experience a religious or spiritual conversion, where their world takes on a transcendent meaning (Joseph 2013).

When the American writer Paul Auster was 14, he was at a summer camp when a boy was struck by lightning and killed. The boy was inches away from Paul, who realised it could have so easily been him. He said, 'I've always been haunted by what happened, the utter randomness of it. I think it was the most important day of my life' (quoted in Laity 2017). Trauma may make us reassess our lives and colour our days for the rest of our lives, as it did for Auster.

PERSONAL STORIES TO HELP THE CHILD AT THE TIME OF BEREAVEMENT

People who have been bereaved in childhood often reflect on what might have helped at the time. Princess Diana died suddenly in a car crash on 31 August 1997 in Paris. She had two young sons, William, aged 15, and Harry, who was 12 at the time. Harry later revealed in an interview that he had grown up thinking not having a mother was normal. He had suppressed his grief at great personal cost (Davies 2017, p.5).

Now aged 33, Prince Harry – with his brother William, the Duke of Cambridge, and his sister-in-law, the Duchess of Cambridge – set up the charity Heads Together. Prince William, visiting Keech Hospice in Luton in 2016, recalled the loss of his mother and the lasting feelings of grief he still has more than 20 years after her death. He reiterated the importance of talking about the person who has died and sharing memories with others. Prince William met Ben Hines at the hospice, whose mother had died the previous year, when she was 40. He urged Ben, his brothers and father to continue talking to each other, commenting that many men are not great sharers and find it hard to talk.

If children are not given the opportunity to explore their loss, to talk about what happened and the impact it has on their lives, it can have major consequences throughout their lives. As with Prince Harry, they feel there was no one to listen and their grief remains submerged but impacts on their lives, emotionally and often physically (Sjoqvist 2007).

ANCESTORS: OUR CONTINUING CONNECTIONS TO THE PAST

Ancestor veneration, which extends respect for elders beyond the grave, is widespread throughout the world (Walter 2017). Hispanic death rites, particularly the Mexican Day of the Dead, combine indigenous and Catholic beliefs. The indigenous belief is that the deceased are ongoing members of the family while Catholic prayers are offered on their behalf.

Although societies are changing, and cultural diversity is often present in our post-industrial world, in Japan the tradition of *sosen suhai* – maintaining connection to the ancestors – continues. The bereaved carry out a series of domestic rites and rituals, which includes the erection of a home altar, a *butsudan*, where the spirit of the dead person can have a home. These family altars provide a direct line to the dead (Klass 1999). The living provide care and comfort for the dead by placing flowers, photographs and personal objects of the deceased on the altar or shrine in the belief that this will facilitate the ancestor's care of the living. Continuing bonds in this way help both the deceased and those who survive them.

In French Polynesia I saw marae structures that represent the seat of spiritual power, in which *Ti'i* or tiki, were placed, symbolic representations of guardian ancestors or gods. Like the enormous statues in Easter Island, tiki were erected to honour significant forebears and ancestors who watched over and guided their descendants. They are of immense importance as they give a spiritual connection to their ancestors. When Captain James Cook came to the islands, he was asked by a Ra'iātea chief for the name of his marae. He thought the chief wanted to know the place 'where our bodies are returned to dust'. However, the marae is 'an essential part of man's social existence, and his relationship to the gods: the question was really, "What place are you particularly identified with and where are your ancestors?"' (Horwitz 2002, p.138).

Recalling the experience of loss, while it may be painful, creates the sense of a continuing presence. We change as we go through the bereavement experience and gradually find ways to invest in the outer world. The raw wound of immediate loss gives way to the scar that remains and will never go away. The healed wound leaves the emotional scar and we remember the pain of loss but can live with the reminder and carry on with our lives. Respecting losses and adversities our ancestors faced can help us to recognise that this is part of all lives, which in turn may help us accept our own losses and bereavements.

LASTING LEGACIES

Doctor, neuroscientist and one of the founders of Doctors without Borders in America, David Servan-Schreiber wrote of his impending death in *Not the Last Goodbye* (2011). The hardest part for him was leaving his wife and three children behind (Duerden 2011). At one point, he reflects on the paternal absence his passing will have, and mentions a soldier from the American Civil War who wrote to his wife before leaving for battle, believing he would not live through the war:

> [And] if he didn't, he hoped that every time she felt a breeze on her face, she would know he was there. I would like to

share that image, that intuition, with my wife and children, so that when they feel the gentle caress of the wind on their faces, they can say: 'Hey, it's Dad, come back to kiss me'. (Servan-Schreiber 2011, p.133)

He completed his powerful book just eight weeks before he died, and it will be a lasting legacy for his bereaved children and all of us who read his words.

In an Afterword, his brother Emile wrote, 'David was not afraid of death. He believed it would transport him to a kingdom of love, through the famous tunnel of light so often described by those who have had a near death experience... You gave us an extraordinary example of what we might call a "successful death experience". A precious parting gift to hold in our hearts, so that, from time to time, we can draw from it some of the strength necessary to confront life' (Servan-Schreiber 2011, p.137).

Chapter 3

KEEPING UP CONVERSATIONS

When someone we love dies, the conversations we have with them do not stop. The person may not be physically with us, but we may continue to speak with them in our internal conversations. In many cases, conversations with the deceased loved one continue for a lifetime. Lucy Dahl's father, the best-selling children's author, Roald Dahl, died when she was 22. Like so many others, including children and young people, she still has conversations with him. Even 26 years after his death she speaks to him all the time. She said that she is always able to find him when she needs him, more so, indeed, than when he was alive. She also meditates every day, asking him for guidance, and asks him questions, which she says he gives answers to – he is an ongoing part of her life.

Children may be reluctant to mention death or talk about dying because they fear that they will make the adults around them uncomfortable or increase their sorrow. They may cover up their own feelings to protect others. They may not talk about dying because they think that by doing so they will make it happen. This 'magical thinking' may continue into adulthood (Didion 2005). However, it is important that we make it safe to talk about this sometimes taboo subject. In clear language, not using euphemisms, we can open up a sensitive dialogue to enable the child to ask the questions they need to ask. These can be quite poignant, for example, 'If Mommy died, does that mean that she won't be here even for my birthday? How can I live the rest of my life without her?' (quoted in Schonfeld and Demaria 2016, e3).

We can help alleviate distress in bereaved children and young people by inviting conversations, expressing concern and offering the space and opportunity to talk about their feelings. In inviting such conversations the child may be sad, but bear in mind that it is the death that has caused the sadness and not the question. If we avoid such conversations the child may believe their grief has not been noticed or is unimportant. Invite discussion with open-ended questions: 'How are you coping since your father died?' 'How are you doing at home since your mother died?'

Listen without judgement and avoid talking about your own experiences unless you truly believe it will help the child. The focus should stay with the child.

THE IMPORTANCE OF COMMUNICATION

In his novel *Grief is the Thing with Feathers* (2015), the author Max Porter includes a section that depicts a child's responses to news about his missing mother:

> We were small boys with remote control cars and ink-stamp sets and we knew something was up. We knew we weren't getting straight answers when we asked 'Where is Mum?' and we knew, even before we were taken to our room and told to sit on the bed, either side of Dad, that something was changed. We guessed and understood this was a new life and Dad was a different type of Dad now and we were different boys, we were brave new boys without a Mum. (Porter 2015, p.133)

Communication is vitally important at all times, but particularly following a bereavement, as Julia Samuel, grief psychotherapist and founder patron of Child Bereavement UK, says in advice to the bereaved: 'Family systems that are "closed" don't have open, honest communications within them. There is less trust and taboo subjects can't be tackled for fear of reprisal' (Samuel 2017, p.91). Open systems inspire trust and ease communication. It is vitally important to listen to the children and young people when someone they love is dying, and also after death. Their voices need to be heard:

> The worst thing is that no one ever asks me how I am coping or if I'm OK. Even though they know what I've been through. My teachers and classmates, they act as if nothing serious has happened to me. (Young survivor of the Japanese Tōhoku earthquake and tsunami, quoted in Suzuki 2011, p.4)

A common theme running through most research into bereavement in childhood is the need for children and young people to be listened to, to be given support and age-appropriate explanations about what has happened (Corr and Balk 2010; Ribbens McCarthy 2006; Tracey 2011). Encourage children to be curious, to ask questions, to keep the conversation going. 'Curious' comes from the Latin 'cura', which means 'to care'. Perhaps, as adults, we can be curious about other people's thoughts and feelings to enable them to share what is important to them. To be curious is to investigate with due diligence. The capacity to listen might be one of our most under-valued human qualities (Fox 1995).

When people, and children, are in the throes of excruciating grief, sharing their pain in talking is one thing that can make a difference that can be critical in the grieving process. Avoidance and lack of recognition of their pain does not help at all. Say you are sorry about the death, say you are sorry that such a terrible event has happened to them, and then ask what you can do to help.

When Kaey was 15, his grandmother died. He missed their conversations. He said, 'At first I visited the cemetery four times a week. It was something to hold on to. I took care of the flowers and sat quietly on the bench next to her grave. I wondered if she could see us and in my mind I kept talking to her.' 'Now,' he added, 'I've realised that life is finite and that you should never waste your time. That's why I am always busy right now. I just don't want to mooch around any more.' He continued, 'Her death still has a big influence on me. It has made think about what matters in life and about what choices to make. In a way it has made me more independent, more grown up' (quoted in Westerink and Stroebe 2013, p.28).

Kaey chose the Vera Lynn wartime song, 'We'll Meet Again', as a way to remember his grandmother and to hold that memory close. He remembers her singing the song, and is quite certain he will meet his grandmother again.

DEATH OF A SIBLING

When a child's sibling dies, it may leave the surviving sibling as an only child, which can be an extremely lonely place to be. Christopher Hall's words accurately reflect this feeling: 'Grief is like being lost. The familiar is gone and we must relearn how to live in the world' (2011, p.7). The ongoing chatter and dialogue between siblings leaves a silence of absence. Keeping up conversations with the dead sibling can ease the sense of loneliness. Conversations can be maintained in drawing or writing, which helps children express their feelings. Encourage the child to express her feelings and to deliver a message to the person who has died, especially if the death was sudden and the child had no time to say goodbye. It might give her the opportunity to say what she was unable to say before the death occurred. This can bring a greater sense of empowerment and control, which is so important in building resilience.

Children may become more insecure after the death of a sibling. They may think that they will die next, contract the same illness or have a similar accident, depending on the cause of death. By clearly communicating about what caused the death, parents can reassure the child that it will not happen to her or that it is very unlikely to happen to her.

Brett was four when his big sister died. He recalls feeling that it was his fault, that he was to blame in some way. He said, 'After Rachael died I had to start school, which I found very difficult because I was convinced something bad would happen to me or someone else if I wasn't with my family' (quoted in CBN 2017). Such feelings are not uncommon, and some bereaved children become school phobic, fearing their absence from home will allow awful things to happen. They may develop separation anxiety and be more clingy. Continued reassurance and helping children voice their fears will be of significant benefit.

Stephen Bank and Michael Kahn wrote a path-breaking book, *The Sibling Bond*, which offers a rare insight into the lives of siblings: 'It has been said that death ends only a life, it does not end a relationship. This statement is especially true when a sibling dies in childhood, adolescence or early adulthood – an untimely death whose unhealthy consequences can endure long after the farewell at the graveside' (1982, p.271). It is not unusual for the impact of death to last for the rest of their lifetime (Devita-Raeburn 2004). Continuing bonds keep the live sibling in touch with the one who died by engaging in specific actions such as thinking of the person, keeping photographs in the home, engaging in conversation and asking the dead sibling for advice and guidance (Packman *et al.* 2006). Many bereaved children believe that the dead sibling is watching over them (Forward and Garlie 2003). This ongoing attachment also includes the anticipation that the siblings will reconnect sometime in the future, usually by a reunion in heaven.

Tabitha was six when her brother Hamish died of a rare form of cancer. Now, 30 years later, she recalled that one of the hardest things to bear was the fact that people assumed that because she was a child, she wouldn't remember him and that it wouldn't affect her. What she still remembers vividly is their time together and the enormous impact it had on her family. The changes that happened in her family 'last forever' and impacted on her throughout her life. She grew up feeling that she had to achieve enough for two (CBUK 2017b).

One study of sibling death, by Helen Rosen, concluded that when there is a critically ill child in the family it often leads to an unintentional form of neglect of the other siblings as the parents unwittingly fail to recognise the changing needs of their healthy children. In a sense, these families are bereaved long before the death takes place, although the feelings of loss, sadness and grief may not be communicated by the children involved. Lois Lowry is the American author of *A Summer to Die*, and her book and comments reflect on this. Her older sister died when Lois was a young girl. When she was writing the book it opened 'the excruciating door of loss' for her. She said her family were WASP (White Anglo Saxon Protestants) and Nordic, and were silent after the death – no one spoke of her sister. A door was closed on the loss, and it was not until she'd written the book, as an adult, when she heard from children and families affected by the book, that she realised that she had sought solace from books. Her comfort was in the stories she read (Lowry 2002).

Not all sibling relationships are amicable. For some the relationship is fraught with conflict and rivalry. After the death of a sibling the remaining one may have feelings of guilt or concern about unfinished business, especially if they did not have the time to say goodbye. In such cases, continuing bonds may not be comforting, and the sense of presence of the dead sibling may be disturbing.

Many children's hospices offer support to the children and young people who have a sibling with a life-limiting illness. Often in such situations the well sibling feels marginalised as their parents spend so much time visiting the sick child in hospital or in a hospice. Their work is underpinned by Article 12 of the United Nations Convention on the Rights of the Child (UNCRC) (UNICEF 1992), which states: 'Children's views must be taken into account in all matters affecting them, subject to the child's age and maturity.' One such hospice, Acorns Children's Hospice Trust in the UK, consulted children and their families to find out what they needed to do to help as their sibling was dying.

The responses from the consultation revealed the struggles of the children and young people. Some siblings felt jealous that their sick brother or sister was getting all the attention, angry that there was little attention paid to them or, as one 15-year-old girl said, 'I really love my brother but sometimes I feel really mad when he has to go back to hospital and everything else just gets forgotten' (quoted in Arens 2006).

Through one-to-one and group work, the siblings felt less isolated and able to have more enjoyable fun times.

Many children with a very sick sibling experience bullying as well as loneliness. As one 15-year-old boy said, 'I have been bullied, the difference with me is because I have a sister with severe disabilities, other pupils see this as a weakness and exploit it' (quoted in Arens 2006).

When a child dies the whole family is affected and the family system changes irrevocably. Everyone in the family experiences a change in their role; for example, if an older sibling dies, the younger one may no longer have a protector or someone to look up to; instead she becomes the only child left for the parents to focus on. This may be particularly difficult if the well sibling believes her parent would have preferred her death rather than the sibling who died. What sustains the sibling after death is where there is a feeling of closeness or sense of togetherness in her family and with her friends. Parental support cannot be underestimated (Packman *et al.* 2006).

As discussed earlier, bereavement may also bring opportunities for growth. After the death of a sibling, many adolescents report psychological growth in the form of increased maturity, higher levels of empathy, feeling more comfortable about death and a greater sense of how to handle adversity. They have an increased awareness of the importance of life, and make every attempt to live life to the full. As Wendy Packman and her colleagues conclude, 'The task of mourning "successfully" is linked to the ability to use continuing bonds in an adaptive ways: Which involves learning from the painful events and building from them in a positive, adaptive way' (Packman *et al.* 2006, p.832).

FUNERALS

Traditionally a funeral is a place where family and friends of the deceased gather to pay their respects and say their farewells to their loved one. It is also a rite of passage, marking the move from life to death, and after the funeral there is often a wake or a social gathering where stories about the dead person are exchanged and memories shared. These conversations may be both revealing and comforting for the bereaved.

Children benefit from being included in the rituals around death, including attending the funeral so they have the opportunity to say goodbye. As in every other aspect of supporting bereaved children, we need to help them make their own decisions and empower them to exert some control over whether or not they attend the funeral (Cranwell 2010). Attending the funeral can also give the young person a completely different perspective on the deceased person. As Ruth said about her mother's funeral, 'I thought, wow, my Mum was really popular! I didn't know she knew so many people! There were people there that I didn't even know' (quoted in Cranwell 2007, p.31). This was a real comfort to her.

Funerals help many bereaved people to accept the reality of a death and to honour the life of the person who has died. If we explain what happens at a funeral and prepare children by answering questions in detail and reassuring them they will be supported by those who care for them, then they can usually relinquish their fears and anxieties about the funeral. Usually they want to take part in memorial or funeral rites with their family but again, they may need to be reassured that the dead person is no longer suffering and no longer feels pain.

Young people who have had an active part to play in the arrangements tend to have strong and positive memories of the funeral, which is helpful in the mourning process. As the novelist Hilary Mantel wrote in an article for *The Guardian*, 'Mourning is work. It is not simply being sad. It is naming your pain. It is witnessing the sorrow of others, drawing out the shape of loss. It is natural and necessary and there is no healing without it' (2017).

My friend Jeanie's mother died when she was seven years old. She told me:

> I was not allowed to go to my mam's funeral. The vision of all black seamed stocking legs with Cuban heeled shoes on

walking round the table, under which I was sitting and had been since they left for the funeral. Or I may have just wanted to hide from everyone, for ever. When they came back from the funeral they didn't know I was there and were saying, 'Poor little thing, what a shame she's so young not to have a mother, especially a little girl. Such a shame, when you think her dad's back now after spending all those six years away from her in the war.'

Now 78, she recalls how it was such a painful experience that it stayed with her for the rest of her life.

Children with Autistic Spectrum Disorder (ASD) may have specific difficulties conceptualising death and the events surrounding death, such as the funeral, and may seem to act in emotionally inappropriate ways (Lipskey 2013; Koehler 2016). These children do grieve, although the lack of expressed emotion may cause difficulties to other members of their family. They may withdraw and become more socially isolated as they strive to understand the feelings and behaviour of people around them. It is helpful to prepare the child for events and to be explicit about what will happen and what their role may be (Schonfeld and Demaria 2016). Euphemisms will confuse a child with ASD even more than neurotypical children. The book *I Have a Question about Death* (2017) by Arlen Grad Gaines, a clinical social worker, and Meredith Englander Polsky, psychologist, National Director of Training and Advocacy at MATLAN, New York, which focuses on the education of Jewish children with special educational needs, is written and illustrated especially for children who are on the ASD spectrum and for others with special needs. It uses straightforward text to explain what happens when someone dies, and other aspects of bereavement and death.

The rituals and rites associated with death are changing, as we can see with current trends in funerals (see, for example, the Co-Operative Funeral Care publication, *The Ways We Say Goodbye*, 2015). According to a survey that they carried out, 50 per cent of people surveyed said that they wanted their favourite song played at their funeral, 26 per cent said they would like mourners to wear bright colours rather than sombre ones, and 80 per cent of funeral directors reported conducting funerals that included a tone of celebration.

Other options bereaved families requested were alternative hearses, such as a glass vintage hearse, a horse-drawn hearse, a motorcycle and sidecar, a Cadillac, an animal or fish-shaped coffin on a cart-based hearse, a cardboard coffin on which friends and family could write their thoughts, messages and last goodbyes to take to the person's final resting place, and a bus or lorry.

Some coffins can be personalised with paintings or pictures on the surface, personal messages placed inside the coffin, and some kind of themed aspect at the funeral. As a bereaved son said:

> My Mum loved Halloween so we chose to wear witch hats and Halloween costumes to pay tribute to her life. Mum was the life and soul so we decided to have a party, not a wake. (Neil Johnson, quoted in Co-Operative Funeral Care 2015)

In some instances, people choose to stream the funeral online so it can be shared with family and friends who may not be able to attend. This also creates a lasting memorial of the event. Young people may take selfies at the funeral of a loved one and post it on social media, since this marks a significant day in their lives that they want to share with others.

To celebrate the life of their mother and the things that she loved, Adam, the husband, commissioned five stained glass panels to insert in the windows above their front door. The bereaved children were included in all the discussions and in the final choices for the window. They included a scene in the Yorkshire Dales where she came from, playing card games, a Christmas scene, poppies and a depiction of their local church. As the sun floods through, lighting up the colours in the windows, the family are reminded of her joy and connection to their ongoing lives.

ONLINE CONVERSATIONS AS CONTINUING BONDS

In our digital age, emerging developments have led to a new area of study, thanatechnology, defined by Carla Sofka, Illene Noppe Cupit and Kathleen Gilbert as, 'All types of communication technology that can be used in the provision of death education, grief counselling and thanatology research' (2012, p.3). Internet-mediated existences are changing how we see death and what happens following death. The funeral industry, forms of memorialisation, the way those who are bereaved communicate with each other and share memories, and the growth of grief counselling online add challenges to the way we work with bereaved children and young people (Sofka *et al.* 2012). Thanablogging, another emerging area, is blogging about death and dying, and gives the opportunity for the dying and bereaved to voice their thoughts and feelings.

Online mourning and memorialisation are increasingly commonplace, and the legacy left on the internet will remain long after the death. A person who uses social media leaves a durable biography. The ongoing uploading and editing of images, text, music and gifts lends vibrancy to the sites where continuing bonds and conversations are maintained (Maddrell 2012). Anyone can contribute to or participate in the making of the ongoing life of a virtual memorial. As their presence is on the internet, they can be visited at any time, night or day, and across the world from anywhere that has internet access.

Many users of memorial sites use them to speak directly to the deceased and to talk to the family and friends of the deceased, especially on significant dates such as birthdays, the anniversary of the death and special days such as Mother's Day.

American Professor of Human Development, Pamela Roberts, has investigated how bereaved people use the internet: 'Those who create web memorials tend to see them as permanent tributes to the dead, providing a place to visit at any time from anywhere and a means to introduce their loved ones to those who never had the chance to meet them' (Roberts 2012, p.55). Pamela Roberts goes on to describe three forms of web memorials: web cemeteries, social networking sites and webrings. Webrings enable personal web pages to be joined together to form a 'ring' that allows the bereaved to be part of a group, with the most numerous concerning the loss of a child or the loss of a pet (Roberts 2012).

There are special memorial sites that can be accessed online such as 1000Memories.com, a social networking site designed for memorialising the dead, the Virtual Memorial Garden,[1] the World Wide Cemetery[2] and www.muchloved.com.

Memorials on places such as Facebook can pose a problem for bereaved young people, however, because of the persistent and openly accessible nature of the site. Conversations on the internet are not always supportive or reasonable; indeed, some can be extremely hurtful and abusive. This may be particularly the case where the death was by suicide (Bell, Bailey and Kennedy 2015), although users assert that continued access to the Facebook accounts of those who have died enables a continued relationship that can give comfort, especially in the early period following bereavement. They also provide an opportunity for the bereaved to give updates on what is happening in their lives. Digital platforms provide the opportunity to post photographs and messages, and are a place to visit as others, in the past, might visit a grave.

The key themes of grieving on social network platforms include a continued bond with the deceased, an online community of those who grieve, giving the opportunity for individual expressions of grief. The digital afterlife brings a form of immortality or an 'enduring biography' (Walter 1996). Digital memories, dates and postings provide an ongoing biography as people add their material to the memorial site. They act as a virtual location for people to share their grief (Bassett 2015). Over time the activity of visiting or maintaining the site decreases, as those who are bereaved

---

1   See www.virtualmemorialgarden.net
2   See http://cemetery.org

reinvest in other aspects of their life and focus less on the death that has happened (Ferris 2016).

DIGITAL LEGACY

A digital legacy is the digital information that is available online about someone following their death. This may include a website, blogs, Facebook, social media profiles, photographs, videos and any number of interactions they had online.

The Digital Legacy Association, founded by James Norris, a research fellow at University College London, was set up to support end-of-life, funeral and palliative care professionals in areas relating to digital legacy and digital assets. DeadSocial. org, also founded by Norris, provides tools, tutorials and resources for the general public. The idea is to empower people to make better end-of-life decisions about their digital legacy and to use technology in this process when an individual needs to do so. As children and young people use social media extensively, a trend that will continue to grow, we may need to help them find support to manage their own or someone else's digital legacy. In Chapter 7 you will find a number of websites that offer online support for children and young people under the heading 'Online forums for connection and conversations'.

CREATIVE APPROACHES TO USE WITH BEREAVED AND GRIEVING CHILDREN

The artist, Michele Angelo Petrone, said 'Paint your feelings. With art there are no rules, everything is valid, you create your own language.' Creative practices for those working with the bereaved can be of immense therapeutic value (Petrone 1999). As research shows, participation in creative activities improves mental wellbeing, social inclusion, decreases emotional distress and can enhance a personal sense of empowerment (All Party Parliamentary Group 2017; Secker *et al.* 2007). Such activities have also been found to give new ways of self-expression, improve self-esteem and provide a rest from distressing feelings, a kind of rest for the grieving mind (Glover *et al.* 2016; Staricoff 2004). The work of Robert Neimeyer, Professor in the Department of Psychology at the University of Memphis, shows how we can engage using a variety of techniques, some of which are explored in the rest of this chapter (Neimeyer 2012; see also Brown 2013).

One of the most useful aspects of creative activities following bereavement is to give respite from grieving, as described by Stroebe and Schut (1999). It is helpful to state that this is important so that the bereaved young person knows explicitly that it is normal and helpful to take a break from mourning, as this aspect of self-care is often overlooked. Also, when engaging in creative activities always ensure that the child feels safe. Never force the child to speak, write or draw if she is not inclined to do so. Respect the child's need to keep quiet when she needs to (Smith and Pennells 1995).

Expressive writing

In *A Grief Observed* (1961, p.50), C.S. Lewis wrote, 'Sorrow turns out to be not a state, but a process. It needs not a map but a history...there is something new to be chronicled every day.' Expressive writing has a long history of being therapeutic and playing a positive role in improving emotional and physical health (Pennebaker 2004). It also helps to boost immune system functioning, which is often compromised after a bereavement (McArdle and Byrt 2001). Writing increases health and wellness in varied ways; as James Pennebaker said, 'there is little doubt that writing has positive consequences. And self-report studies suggest that writing about emotional topics is associated with significant reductions in distress' (Pennebaker 1997, p.162).

We can help children or young people express their feelings in practical, creative activities. They can write about what happened, draw their family before and after the death, draw how they see their future or what makes them feel safe at the moment. Providing a structure in group or in individual sessions helps them express their thoughts and feelings.

Structure may come in the form of lists, acrostics, themes, journeys, family stories or anniversaries. Those taking part may be surprised by the pleasant memories that emerge from the activity rather than predominantly sad emotions. If someone finds it difficult to express themselves, a word or time limit or a specific task can reduce early anxieties (Graves 2009).

Activities for children or young people to help in their writing might include:

- Write about a cherished memory of a loved one who has died.

- Write about things they did together...at home...at the hospice...

- Write about something a loved one taught them to do.

- What is their special memory object of their loved one?

- Ask them to choose a stone and with a permanent marker to write words on it that they think will help people to carry on after the death of someone close.

Expressive writing can be particularly useful at a time of transition, such as a bereavement or at a later point in life when the young person wants to explore what the death meant to her. When she was eight years old Sarah Fitzgerald's sister died in a road crash. At first it felt unreal and hard to take in; although she was offered counselling at school, she was too numb to take advantage of it. She felt lonely and said that she cried a lot because she felt so angry. When she was 11 she accessed support from a counsellor at Acorns Children's Hospice Trust in Birmingham, and found she wanted to express her feelings in writing. She wrote an allegory about two dolphins as she couldn't write directly about her sister, and they had both loved dolphins. The book was published under the title *The Tale of Two Dolphins: When My Sister Died Suddenly* (1999). Sarah felt that the writing helped her; she slept better and was more sociable. Now professionals use the book to help others who have suffered sudden bereavement. Sarah said that adults sometimes don't listen, that they do things differently. Her book shows how you can be happy a long time after something terrible has happened, but still be sad at the same time. She said that she has received many letters from children saying that this is exactly how they felt (Mistiaen 1999).

Poetry

Zelda Fitzgerald, American socialite, painter, novelist and wife of F. Scott Fitzgerald, said, 'No one has ever measured, not even poets, how much the heart can hold' (quoted in Campanella 2011, p.193) Nobel Literature prize-winning poet Seamus Heaney was bereaved when he was a teenager. His poem, 'Mid-Term Break', describes how he was told of the death of his four-year-old brother Christopher who was killed by a car in 1953. The intensely biographical poem charts the impact of loss and grief and is one of the most moving poems about the death of a sibling ever written. The verse expresses the pain, and untimeliness, of early death. Heaney writes that Christopher's coffin is like a cot, four foot long, in which each foot of length represents a year of his young life. The only sign of injury is a small bruise, the colour of a poppy.

When Heaney died he was buried beside his brother in the graveyard adjoining St Mary's Church, Bellaghy, Northern Ireland. The bond with his brother was never broken.

As the elegiac nature of Heaney's 'Mid-Term Break' commemorates the death of his brother, young people might want to write an elegy about their loved one who has died as a way of remembering them and of celebrating their life.

Many artists put their experience of grief into their creative work. Poet Emily Berry explored the loss of her mother in a moving collection of poems called *Stranger, Baby*. Through her writing she attempts to gain control over her feelings. Her poems show how feelings, once written down, can become art. Poems provide a new lens with which to consider grief. Berry writes in the acknowledgements that the book is in memory of her mother (2017).

Journal writing

A journal can act as a reliable companion, one who receives your thoughts and feelings without judgement and with no interruptions (Hoyle 2012). The safe haven of the blank pages allows the writer to weather the storms and flurries of grief, and can be a kind of sanctuary. The act of writing can contain negative emotion and modify it positively. In addition, a journal is portable – you can take it with you wherever you go. It can also reflect who we were, who we are and who we are becoming as we make our transition following the death of a loved one. The bereaved can learn so much from free, expressive writing. As Robert Neimeyer reflects, '...lessons of loss, when integrated, can help people move from post-traumatic *stress* to post-traumatic *growth*' (quoted in Hoyle 2012, p.97).

Keeping a journal can be like having a listening friend who is there for you whenever you choose to make contact (Moss 2012). Children and young people may find that recording their thoughts and feelings in a private journal allows them to express themselves more easily than talking. It can bring flashes of clarity and self-awareness, and may be an impetus to make positive changes as the young people move through their experience of loss. It is a place where anger and frustration can be safely expressed (Gray 2011).

A grief journal can be a way of finding our way through our feelings and can help us to recognise that when we feel anger, it is our grief speaking; when we write about fear, it is our grief speaking; and when we write about guilt, it is our grief speaking. We can recognise that in giving words to our pain we honour it and give it its proper place out in the open, where it is acknowledged. The more we run from grief or cower away from it, the larger it can become.

For some young people journal writing can act as a continuing bond to the person they loved. They may write to them telling them what is going on in their lives and keep them up to date with new relationships. They may also write letters to them. As time passes, re-reading what they have written may show them how their grief has changed over the months and years.

Often in bereavement young people find it hard to concentrate, particularly on school work. Getting thoughts down on paper is one way of managing them. By writing in a journal, the thoughts and emotions can be written down to clear a space in the mind, creating a temporary reprieve from the myriad of feelings the child or young person is feeling.

Mind mapping

Mind mapping is a technique that can help children and young people make sense of their feelings and experiences. It can also lead on to some creative problem-solving and reveal healing potentials.

In this example, the young person puts the central event, her father's death, in the middle of the paper, and then writes the feelings and concerns as they orbit the death:

These, in turn, can be made into extended maps. For example, the child prioritises 'Scared something will happen to Mum', and repeats the process:

The mind map gives something tangible to hold on to, and it is the process of putting thoughts and fear onto paper which is itself healing. It also gives the child the opportunity to look at how bereavement spills over into so many aspects of her life. It gives the young person the chance to prioritise what is most important to her to address and to regain control. It can help develop an open conversation with bereaved young people and give them a sense of achievement as they look at their difficulties and find ways to feel better. This creative technique helps build self-esteem and resilience, which are so important for bereaved young people whose confidence can be affected by bereavement.

Autobiographical art

As Nietzsche said, 'Art takes an ice pick to the heart' (quoted in Samuel 2017, p.78). Autobiographical art specifically includes the experiences of the maker. Cathy Phelan, an artist, made a full size model of a horse after her husband, Daniel, died. The frame was covered with notes the couple had sent to each other, personal cards that were sent to him, part of a report from his therapist, shopping lists and a number of doodles that Daniel loved to do. For Cathy it was a visible expression of their relationship and the strength she felt he had as he went through his cancer treatment (Mitchell 2017).

Collage work

Taking inspiration from Phelan's work, we can use this creative approach with children. Encourage them to use images, written letters, notes, sketches, hospital car park tickets – anything they like – to make an autobiographical collage. Choose whatever size of paper or card that is most appropriate for the age and confidence of the child. Also, instead of a flat collage, you could make an indoor tree using branches from which to hang personal notes and memorabilia. This type of creativity is good for the kind of concentration that comes with mindfulness, and brings the opportunity for reflection. Sometimes the chance to quietly create something is a balm to the sadness and the tiredness that comes with grieving.

Following the death of her brother, Meika, a Japanese woman, wanted to reconnect to him and express her grief in a non-traditional manner, so she made a series of collages. She said, 'I wanted to try and connect with my brother and heal my sadness. The feeling I had was that by making this, that somehow he was returning to me' (quoted in Valentine 2009, p.11).

Worry dolls

The indigenous people of Guatemala, South America, have a tradition of making 'worry dolls'. These small dolls are kept in a pouch or special box, and when a child is worried she can take out a doll, at bedtime, for example, tell it her worry and put it under her pillow so that the doll can resolve her trouble as she sleeps. Usually there are six dolls so the child can have a maximum of six worries to share at any one time. You can help the grieving child to make the little dolls or draw them on card and colour them in. These dolls can also be bought.

Paper boats

Make paper boats and place candles or tea lights in them and sail them on a pond. The child can write or draw images to place in the boat. The symbol of light in the darkness is enabling and reassuring, which is why it is a good activity to do at dusk.

Knitted squares – a blanket of love

In Australia, through 'Good Grief' adventure-based camps, set up by the National Association for Loss and Grief (NALAG), bereaved children are helped to find ways to cope with their loss. Each weekend concludes with a 'Love Wrap' ritual. Made of woollen squares knitted by Elders who had experienced grief themselves, each blanket symbolises the child's unique grief – no two blankets are the same. The blanket is taken home to keep the child safe on their grief journey. These 'Love Wrap' rituals reinforce bonds with the Elders in the community and represent continuing bonds with the ancestors in their culture who have also undergone loss and the impact of death. The links between the generations are reinforced by these powerful rituals.

Glass beads memory vase

Children and young people choose different coloured beads and fill a vase with layers of colours. They begin by first talking about what each colour means for them or what it represents for the person who has died. For example, blue may signify loyalty and dependability, yellow for warmth and kindness, red for energy, love and passion, grey for sorrow and the dark clouds that sometimes come. As the child makes layers in the vase she may talk about what each layer represents.

The vase can be kept dry, or filled with water, possibly with the addition of flowers. If the vase is dry you could add a candle that can be lit on special anniversaries or when the bereaved child wants to remember her connection with the deceased person. Offer the child choices to create what she wants. This is part of the process of enabling children to assert some control in their world, which is empowering and a positive way to enhance resilience.

Landscape of loss

Using clay make a landscape with the child that describes the loss. This activity is probably better done with closed eyes. Let the landscape emerge, then help the child to think about what feelings or times it represents. If you have small toys, such as animals or characters, the child may place them in her landscape and tell the story of what she is doing or feeling.

A bunting of memories

Make a series of triangles of different colours with the child and, in indelible ink, ask her to write a message or memory on each piece of fabric. Simple words used to describe the dead person can be included: funny, fierce, loving, clever, quick tempered, brave, warm – whatever words the child wants to use. The bunting can be hung somewhere that is significant for the child, including in a garden or a bedroom.

Keeping up conversations and maintaining continuing bonds for bereaved children and young people is a vital aspect of grief work. By helping them with this task in a creative way, we can elicit strengths that can bring both compassion for themselves and others as well as resilience in living the life they want to live (Staricoff 2004).

Chapter 4

GUIDING LIGHTS: DREAMS AND SPIRITUALITY

Dreaming and spirituality are often overlooked when working with bereaved children and young people, yet they are integral aspects of human life. Everyone dreams, although they may not remember them, and most people search for meaning in their lives, including children. Some define spirituality as a quest for new meaning (Batten and Oltjenbruns 1999), which is what happens after bereavement as we seek to find meaning in what has happened to us (Neimeyer, Baldwin and Gillies 2006).

Dreaming is a universal language that speaks to us directly or in symbols and metaphor. It is a universal human experience, and the emotions experienced in dreams spill over into waking life, which is why it is a good idea to regularly ask children how they slept and to ask about their dreams. This provides an opportunity for them to communicate their feelings and anxieties, especially after they have been bereaved. In cultures where dreams are seen as important, the bereaved are more likely to talk about their dreams.

DREAMS AND NIGHTMARES

When a child has been bereaved his dreams may reflect the impact of this seismic event in his life. If we care for children, we must also care about their dreams and help them to harness their healing power. As they grow, children learn that dreams are linked to their own waking experiences rather than coming from outside themselves, for instance, coming from their pillow (Mallon 1989). Noted bereavement researcher, J. William Worden states, 'Children who maintained a connection with the (deceased) parent through dreams and feeling watched knew, for the most part, that these experiences were coming from somewhere inside themselves' (1996, p.29).

Nightmares, those distressing, frightening dreams that often wake children up in the middle of the night, are usually prompted by disturbing waking events. In a sense, they are literally a 'wake-up' call, to draw attention to some aspect of life that is troubling us. In children, it may be a personal event in the family, neglect, abuse or some kind of external threat (Bulkeley and Bulkeley 2016). Many children experience recurring nightmares that do not stop until the underlying issues have been addressed and resolved. In responding to nightmares, we need to comfort and reassure the child that they are normal, and that nearly every child will have a nightmare at some point.

CHILDREN'S DREAMS FOLLOWING BEREAVEMENT

Dreams, nightmares, communication with the deceased and symbolic representation of events surrounding death are common elements in the mourning process. Children's dreams frequently reveal the continuing bonds that connect the child to the person who has died. They also show that grieving does not have a finite time limit. In fact, 'the dead are a positive resource to be drawn on by the living' (Riches and Dawson 2000, p.37). Dreams as a form of continuing bond have been found in many studies (see, for example, Ishida *et al.* 2010; Krause and Bastida 2010). The following example shows how such dreams give a form of communication with someone who has died:

> I have dreams with my father. Maybe four or five dreams since he died. When I have the dreams I am very happy. I have a

lot of joy to see him and talk to him. Right now, I have the opportunity to tell him in the dreams that I love him very much, and I didn't tell [him] this before, when he was alive. (Quoted in Foster *et al.* 2012, p.125)

A number of studies have found overlapping categories of activities in dreams following bereavement. In the dreams the deceased deliver messages to the bereaved and give them the chance to say goodbye (Barrett 1992). In many cases the dead telephone their loved one, or the setting of the dream is a place of transition. They meet by a garden gate, a barrier at an airport or at a threshold of some kind. Frequently, a dream message may be delivered in diverse forms – by text, by letter, in person or on a computer screen – or the message may be transferred without words into the mind of the bereaved young person. These messages may bring a surprise, although more often the dreamer delivers a message to himself via the image of the deceased person. These dreams also help the bereaved accept the reality of death (Garfield 1997).

Dreams relating to bereavement may occur before death as a form of anticipatory grief, and children who are living with a terminally ill member of their family may have dreams that are distressing. Emotional arousal affects the intensity of the child's dreams (Hartman and Basile 2003), and he may be fearful about what will happen to him after the death takes place. It is important to support the child by talking about his fears, offering whatever reassurances can be given, and to help him communicate his feelings to those around him. Silence and lack of inclusion isolate the child and hamper the grief process.

Dreams may also come immediately after the death of a loved one as a reaction to the loss, and dreams of the deceased may occur for the rest of the child's lifetime, reflecting the nature of his relationship with the deceased (Klass *et al.* 1996). Where children dream of death or have death-related dreams this may link to a fear of being abandoned: 'What would happen if my mother died? Who would take care of me?' (Lewis 1961). C.S. Lewis talks about 'fear fulfilment' dreams as well as the more familiar, wish fulfilment dreams (Lewis 1961, p.35).

Where the deceased loved one appears in a dream, the child may be pleased with the connection, although he may feel sad when he wakes up to find the person is not physically present. However, research has shown that dreaming facilitates the mourning process. When the deceased returns to life in the dream it allows past and present to be integrated (LoConto 1998; Mallon 2011). In my experience children and young people have a vivid dream life after bereavement. Their assumptive world has been shaken and their subconscious continues to try to make sense of the event and to come to terms with it as they sleep. Grieving is not a linear process, and bereaved children will revisit the death and the circumstances surrounding it at different points in their life, and their dreams will reflect this.

DREAM THEMES

Children often experience nightmares between the ages of three and sixteen. Common themes concern being separated from people they love and trust, symbolically representing the separation they have experienced through death:

> The most frightening dream I have had is about my sister on her tricycle riding on to the road and someone sees her and takes her away and I can't stop thinking about that. (Umza, nine years old)

After a major loss, the kidnapping or disappearance of another family member or friend often relates to a fear, usually unspoken, that another loss will take place.

Another theme is being abandoned, left behind or deserted and being attacked, injured or violated in some way:

> Mum was going away because she didn't want to live at home anymore. Then everyone in the family was going. I followed them. They went to the motorway, then I got lost. They left me behind. There was no one to look after me. (Javed, eight years old)

Dreams may also include being separated from the deceased loved one and of seeing them, but not being able to reach them. Such dreams reveal the desire to reconnect but being unable to do so. The child yearns for the dead person but cannot join him or her.

A common theme is of being overwhelmed by uncontrollable events such as a flood, fire or avalanche. These themes reflect the powerlessness children and young people feel following bereavement (Mallon 2011). They symbolise the overwhelming events that they are facing in anticipating a death or following a bereavement.

Shapeshifting dreams, in which a familiar person transforms into a frightening person or animal, are not uncommon (Mallon 2002). Such dreams show us how children recognise at a deep level the duality of human beings. A dream of his mother who changes into a fearful witch, for example, may reflect the fact that the child understands that his mother has a negative side to her nature as well as a loving, caring side. We, humans, are full of complexities, and one of the jobs of childhood is to learn about this.

Mina, 14, had the following dream:

> Some people came to my house, I offered them some tea then they turned into wolves. We try to escape. Outside everyone else is turning into wolves. I see my closest friend Yasmin, and to my horror, I see she is turning into a wolf.

This shapeshifting dream reflected Mina's concerns about dangerous strangers and racist behaviour she had experienced. Who could she trust? Even her friends might be a threat to her.

TRAUMA AND DREAMS

In my work as a bereavement counsellor I have seen many children who have experienced the devastation of a traumatic death. Jessie, for example, was six when her older brother Emile was hit by a van as he tried to cross the road. He was following their older brother Timothy. Jessie did not see the accident that killed her brother, but the whole family was overwhelmed by the pain of his death and the shock and horror that Timothy had felt as he witnessed the death of his brother and was unable to save him. Timothy felt survivor guilt, and that it would have been better if he had died rather than his younger brother. Jessie, enmeshed in the grief of her family, was having bad dreams and was sleeping poorly.

Jessie was fearful about going to sleep because of frightening dreams. She told me of one dream: 'I dreamt a lion came into my bedroom and ate Emile. I couldn't stop the lion.' She was on the verge of tears. When I asked her to draw the dream, she drew a huge lion with Emile clenched between his large teeth while she cowered to the side. After we talked about how the dream was frightening, I asked Jessie if she would like to change the dream. With a sense of reprieve she drew another picture in which her brother overcame the lion and was safe. Emile, in the picture, had a huge smile, and Jessie stood happily by his side. Jessie and I met another couple of times and she was sleeping well. Although she missed her brother, she knew that he was there in her dreams and her thoughts, and she still maintained a bond with him. She also knew that she could draw happier endings where a dream was upsetting. She had the tools to regain some control, which empowered her.

In exploring dreams following bereavement we can use creative approaches such as drawing, painting, writing about them and acting out the different characters in the dreams. We can develop different storylines and introduce helpers to assist the dreamer, as happens in the hero's journey we touched on in Chapter 2. As we empower children to gain greater control of their dreams in their waking life, their dreams usually become less distressing because they have addressed their fears in waking life.

Ten-year-old Helena's father died by suicide. When she first found out she was shocked, frightened to do anything new, and felt tired all the time. She dreamt that he was still alive and was sad when she woke up to find he was not alive. Grieving is so exhausting, and I was able to reassure her that how she was feeling was something lots of people feel after someone they love has died (Vercoe and Abramowski 2004). She was worried about going back to school and telling people how her father had died. Even at the age of ten she felt the stigma that is still attached to death by suicide. However, when she accepted that she was not to blame for his death, and understood that he had had many very troubling events happening in his life that led him to think his family would be better off without him, she felt some relief. She came to understand that he had rejected his life, but not her.

Adults who care for suicidally bereaved children and young people can ensure that they understand that the death was not their fault. They also need to be told the truth about the death, taking into account their age and level of understanding or maturity (Trickey 2005). Helena was still sad, but with a very loving, stable mother who listened to her and kept her safe, she could rebuild her life while continuing to love her father and prize the bonds she maintained with him.

VISITATION DREAMS

Dreams in which the deceased 'visit' the bereaved child or young person are part of the continuing bond that they experience. Visitation dreams are often very intense and feel different from ordinary dreams. They have been recorded throughout history and across cultures (Adams, Hyde and Wooley 2008; Bulkeley 2000; Mallon 2002). Such dreams may bring great comfort or distress to the dreamer.

The following two examples show how each child found comfort from their visitation dreams:

> In my dream, all the family were at the crematorium, my granddad had died. The coffin was just about to disappear behind the curtains. The vicar was just saying, 'Now Sydney G. is to be cremated.' Just then there came a croaking noise from the coffin. It started to open and Granddad got out of it. And, after that everything was alright. (Maxwell, nine years old)

> In reality my father died nearly six years ago of leukaemia. I dreamt not long ago that the doorbell went and he was

standing on the doorstep with all his cases ready to come home. (Justine, 15 years old) (Quoted in Mallon 1998)

Maxwell told his mother and father about the dream and they had a conversation about his grandfather's death and how they felt about their loss. Maxwell said that he knew Granddad was now happy in heaven with Granny, but he just wished he could still be with them (quoted in Mallon 1998). Like so many young people, Maxwell believed that the dead live on in an afterlife, which is often in heaven (Bulkeley and Bulkley 2005).

Justine's dream can be seen as a wish fulfilment dream. She understands that her father cannot come back to the physical body and life he had before his death, but she feels he is part of her world. In addition, she knows he did not want to die and would have stayed with her if his illness had not caused his death.

Award-winning musician Sir Paul McCartney had a dream that inspired his song 'Let It Be' after he saw his mother in a dream. The lyrics include the words 'Mother Mary comes to me.' He dreamt of his own deceased mother, although many listeners thought it was a Biblical reference. The visit in his dream reflected the ongoing bond he has with his mother.

THE SPIRITUAL DIMENSION OF DREAMS

Many cultures hold the belief that when we dream, our spirit can leave our body and travel in different dimensions. Australian Aborigines believe that dreams free us from the limitations of time and space, and in them they can meet ancestors who give them advice and bring them wisdom. The Narranga-ga tribe say that the human spirit can leave the dreamer's body and travel to make contact with other spirits, including those of the dead (Mallon 2000).

Shamans in all traditions see dreams as a means to travel between worlds:

It was dark and suddenly I saw a light, all sparkly. It was a big angel with big wings. She smiled at me and said that Nana was with her drinking a cup of tea and Nana was very happy. When I woke up, I was happy because I knew I would see Nana again one day with the angels. She always drinks tea but I don't like tea. It was a special dream. (Oliver, seven years old, quoted in Adams 2016)

Many children have dreams that seem particularly significant. These are big dreams that may be remembered for all of their life. Swiss psychiatrist C.G. Jung described these as numinous dreams, sacred and profound. The transcendent nature of such dreams may bring comfort, especially after a traumatic death such as manslaughter or a sudden death in a traffic collision (Brake 2011).

Pattie, a seven-year-old Roman Catholic girl in Northern Ireland, who was part of a film I made called 'Children Dreaming' for a BBC Inside Stories series, told me about her very special dream:

I dreamt I was in heaven with all the other angels. Jesus was welcoming me. I was so happy and God asked me if I wanted to be his helper and I said 'Yes'.

She beamed as she recounted the dream, and said it made her the happiest person alive.

Christianity, Judaism and Islam refer to divine dreams in their religious texts, as do other world religions. For her doctoral research, Kate Adams collected 107 reports of dreams from children about God or dreams that they believed came from God or Allah. The children had secular, Christian or Muslim upbringings, and were aged between nine and twelve. She writes, 'This study illustrates that when a child suggests that they have had a dream from God, this is not necessarily a matter to be dismissed as "immature thinking". Instead many children offer mature and articulate explanations to support their claims, as well as providing interpretations of their dreams, which are often insightful' (Adams 2004, p.7).

Angels, in many cultures, are seen as spiritual beings who mediate between God and human beings. Martin Grimmitt and his colleagues wrote a book, *A Gift to the Child* (1991), in which a teacher talked about how moved she was after she and her primary school class had done a project on dreams. She said:

> There is such a bond between me and the children now after the angels work and we shared our dreams. The children are more ready to talk about their beliefs, their inner selves, much more willing to share on a deeper level than before. Many parents have noticed it too, how the children have been so open, so frank about things. The benefits are intangible but so great and go on and on. (Grimmitt, Grove and Spencer 1991, quoted in Mallon 2002, p.158)

Given the opportunity and a space in which compassionate listening can take place, children and young people will talk about their deepest feelings that are evoked by their dreams.

Children have told me about dreaming of a guardian angel who is taking care of them or who is looking after deceased relatives. These dreams make the child feel protected and cared for, and bring much solace after bereavement. Sometimes they are called 'divine dreams', whether they have specific religious links or spiritual themes that are unrelated to any faith tradition (Adams 2016). Such dreams may feature God, Allah or a god-like figure, or the dreamer thinks they have been sent by God and have a divine message for them.

Ashley was 13 years old when she told me of a dream:

> When I was about five years old I was ill and I dreamt that an angel appeared in the room and my mother explained to her about my illness. She gave a blessing and I was instantly cured. In reality I was a little better after the dream.

Dying children sometimes speak of relatives who are waiting for them 'on the other side'. As Elisabeth Kübler-Ross, a Swiss-American psychiatrist who worked extensively with children on the cusp of death, says, 'every single child who mentioned that someone was waiting for them mentioned a person who had actually preceded them in death, even if by only a few moments. And yet none of these children had been informed of the recent death of the relatives by us at any time'

(1985, p.110). She firmly believed that dreams of the dead are contacts on a spiritual plane (Kübler-Ross 1975).

HEAVEN

Heaven is a source of comfort for many children and young people brought up in the Christian tradition. For others, heaven is a good place to go to eventually, but in this child's view, not too soon. A mother told a radio station the following story:

> I have two children aged three and five, and after my father died they were one day with my mother when the three-year-old asked, 'What happened to Grandpa when he died?' Before my mother could answer, her five-year-old brother answered, 'God came down as Superman and carried him off to heaven.' 'In that case,' said his sister, 'When you die Granny and Superman comes to get you, I shall hang on to your feet.' (Quoted in Waskett 1995, p.45)

SPIRITUALITY

> *I slept and dreamt that life was joy. I awoke and saw that life was service. I acted and behold, service was joy.*
>
> Rabindranath Tagore, 1861–1941
> (quoted in Jacobs 1991)

Spirituality is often seen as an integral part of the human condition and is found across cultures. It does not have to be linked to the religious beliefs, although it may be (Bellous 2010; Hay and Nye 2006). It is usually defined as that which relates to or affects the human spirit or soul as opposed to material or physical things. Spiritual experiences are when we feel most deeply connected to our world, and when we feel part of something much greater than our own ego. Such transcendent experiences often leave a person with a sense of being part of the universe, being linked to the rest of humankind, and of feeling a profound connection with the purpose and meaning of life (Bosacki 2001).

Spiritual needs are present in everyone, although we may have varying spiritual needs depending on who we are and what we believe our purpose in life is. As people approach death, the spiritual dimension of their existence may become more central to their thoughts as they contemplate what their life meant and whether they completed what they wanted to do. Cultural and spiritual beliefs will also influence how the terminally ill person and their family understand death and how they cope with it. Many people who have strong religious beliefs find comfort in the idea of the presence of a higher power in their life. If people believe there is life after death, then death can be seen as a new beginning (Bull 2007).

We need to give children and young people the opportunity to express their feelings about God, faith, religion or spirituality. There is still some kind of reluctance in society to talk about spirituality, so children and young people sensing this do not talk about their own thoughts and feelings on the subject. However, for some, their faith and religion is a great comfort. Bereavement is a life crisis that challenges assumptions and provides the grounds for spiritual change (Balk 1999). Having a sense that there is something bigger than the world we live in, a spirituality that brings meaning to one's life, can dramatically change our priorities about what is important to us. This aspect of spirituality can act as a guiding light for young people, especially those who have experienced bereavement. It can lead to post-traumatic growth, as we saw earlier.

Children's author Mark Lemon had a tragic experience when he was 12. His father was murdered. The trauma of his father's death left Mark struggling throughout his teenage years; however, it brought important growth for him in later life. He said, 'I hope that in some way my experience has taught me to enjoy life and love my family even more; it has certainly given me an outlook on life that can only come from losing someone so precious. It has made me stronger, both for myself and my family' (Lemon 2017). He also said that he always believed that his father continued to guide him through his life, a view shared by many bereaved young people and adults.

We live in a society in which there are many faiths, belief systems, ethnic diversity and a vast number of rites and rituals that accompany life and death. In Manchester, where I live, the recent devastating atrocity at the Manchester Arena caused the death of 22 victims and serious, life-changing injuries to many more. The crowd, mainly young people, who had gone to see the singer Ariana Grande, were caught in a situation they could not have imagined. In the days following the attack, Mancunians rallied to reject the hatred and ignorance of its perpetrators. The vigils reflected the multicultural nature of the city and the many faiths followed. Believers and non-believers shared the space to honour the dead and to show compassion to the families and friends of all affected by the tragedy.

There is a spiritual dimension to grief that is influenced by the faith, belief or spiritual practices within the home and community. This is reflected in books for children and young people. In Judy Pascoe's novel, *Our Father Who Art in a Tree* (2003), her main character, Simone, says: 'It was simple for me: the saints were in heaven, and guardian angels had extendable wings like Batman, and my dad had died and gone to live in the tree in the backyard' (2003, p.1). She is convinced that her father's spirit had moved to the tree where she could go and sit in the branches and listen to him. She thought that if you climbed high enough, you could reach another world. Many bereaved children believe that another world exists where spirits go after death, which is a view written about in numerous sagas, myths and folklore traditions throughout the world.

Sibling bereavement may be a catalyst for spiritual development in adolescents as they struggle to find new meaning in their life (Batten and Oltjenbruns 1999).

The emotional and spiritual lives of children with learning disabilities are often overlooked or ignored as family and carers focus on daily tasks and routines. However, it is important to consider the emotional life of each child, otherwise they are disenfranchised and further disabled (Blackman 2003; Mallon 1998).

The child's family and wider social network will influence his view of what happens after death, and will be reinforced by the religious or secular world he inhabits. Klass (1999, p.41) recognised that: 'Inner representations of the dead and continuing bonds are not simply individual matters. They are maintained and reinforced in families and within wider social systems.' An example of this is the Day of the Dead, celebrated annually in Mexico in November. A public holiday, the day is devoted to praying for and remembering those who have died. Some families build private altars, *ofrendas*, on which they place candles, food, flowers and possessions of the deceased. In cemeteries family members invite dead relatives to descend from heaven on special ladders made from bread dough to join them. Families bring picnics, celebrate their ancestors and share favourite foods. At the end of the day, the dead go back to heaven using the ladder until they return the next year (Way 2010). As in so many societies across the world, the dead are remembered and honoured in rites and rituals as the living reinforce their continuing bonds with those who have died.

NEAR DEATH EXPERIENCE

Many people have reported on a powerful experience as they hovered between life and death or had clinically died but been resuscitated (Fenwick and Fenwick 1995). The characteristics of a near death experience (NDE) are a tunnel or passage towards light, light that is filled with love and compassion, an out-of-body experience (OOBE), a sense of great peace, joyousness, the presence of deceased relatives or friends waiting and welcoming them, a strong desire to stay with them and a strong reluctance to return to their physical body. In many cases, there is a life review as the person sees a series of events that have happened prior to the NDE. Dr David Servan-Schreiber describes one patient's experience of near death: 'She was in a tunnel, and at the end of this tunnel was a soothing white light that drew her towards it. But, it wasn't her time, and with regret she had to turn back and return to her poor damaged body' (2011, p.106).

It is estimated that between 8 and 15 per cent of a population, depending on the country, have a NDE. Researcher Dr Elizabeth Fenwick and neuropsychiatrist Peter Fenwick wrote of their findings in *The Truth in the Light: An Investigation of Over 300 Near-Death Experiences* (1995). It includes numerous accounts of children who have had a NDE, including the NDE characteristics noted earlier. Although there are many explanations about why these phenomena happen, in terms of this section on spirituality, almost everyone says that thanks to the experience, they no longer feared death. They generally saw the light as Jesus, God or Divine Love. Having seen deceased loved ones 'on the other side', they also believed that there was some kind of afterlife in a paradise full of light.

According to P.M.H. Atwater, a North American writer and researcher, 'Those who have had near death experiences, including children, develop a renewed spiritual understanding which may contradict the religious views they were brought up with' (1999, p.42). Claire, an 11-year-old girl living in the UK, had a dream when she was eight after her friend died. There was 'this big golden tunnel; and I was walking through it and she was at the end of it, and I was talking to her and I said, "what's happening?"' They carried on a brief conversation, Claire's friend telling her about how happy she was in the new place with new friends, and Claire telling her what was happening at school. Claire called the tunnel the 'gate to heaven' (quoted in Adams and Hyde 2008), although her experience occurred in a dream and was not a NDE. The transcendent dimension of the dream was a great comfort to Claire.

Many people undergo a complete spiritual transformation after a NDE. As physicist David Darling says in his book, *Soul Search*, 'for many indeed, the near-death experience stands as the most powerful and convincing testimony yet for the existence of an afterlife' (1995, p.41). These spiritual aspects help to develop compassion, gratitude and altruism, all qualities that help heal at times of transformation (Emmons and McCullough 2003).

> An NDE is an accelerated spiritual transformation –
> these people have literally encountered death in a totally
> unexpected and sudden way. It has taken something to shake
> the foundations of their being and to experience life in ways
> other than what they have been conditioned to believe.
> (Sartori 2014, p.184)

The meetings with deceased relatives in NDEs once again
point to continuing bonds between the living and the dead.
That connection can be a source of spiritual nourishment:
'The prospect of joining the entire community of human and
animal souls in a universe that is bathed in light, connectedness
and love, fills me with joy' (Servan-Schreiber 2011, p.111).

AFTERLIFE

Children have many views about what happens after death.
These are obviously influenced by their families, culture,
education and the wider society in which they live. Anita
Moorjani, a *New York Times* best-selling author, writes in her
book *Dying to Be Me*:

> Because of my Hindu roots...I grew up to believe in karma
> and reincarnation. Most Eastern religions are based on
> these laws, believing that the purpose of life is to raise our
> consciousness and spirituality and evolve through each cycle
> of birth and death to the point of reaching enlightenment.
> At that point, we break the cycle of birth and death and no
> longer need to reincarnate into a flesh and blood body. That
> state is called *nirvana*. (2012, p.15)

In working with children it is important to discover what their
beliefs are and to respect them. These will form part of the
fabric of their lives which sustain them through uncertain
times, especially after the death of someone close. As we saw
earlier, NDEs may convince children that there is a place
that transcends our world, where we can, once again, meet
deceased loved ones. Whether this is heaven, paradise or a
place of light, it has a profound impact on the continuing life
of the child.

Chapter 5

LOVING YOURSELF WHEN SOMEONE YOU LOVE HAS DIED

For a child to love themselves after someone has died can be very difficult as the child may be flooded with diverse emotions.

The following young people told me how it felt for them following bereavement (taken from my case studies):

> Angry things kept buzzing in my mind. When you're a teenager, just when everything's starting to happen in your life then it is reduced to cinders suddenly. I felt guilty because of this anger, and just continue and manage these big things at the same time. Then I felt I must protect my mother and brother because they needed me. (Sarah, 15 years old; her father had died in a car crash)

> I didn't feel anything for the first three months. For the next six to eight months I couldn't really handle myself or my feelings. Then after that it took me a long time and a lot of tears but I managed to calm down. Ever since then it's been like a long road up a hill. (Helen, 14 years old; her father died by suicide)

Bereavement does not go away. It is a difficult but integral part of the normal life cycle that we all share. It is a period of loss, of change, and is a period of transition. It involves the bereaved's relationship to herself, to the deceased and to others in her community and world. Our relationships with others, living or dead, frame our sense of self and how we live. The past, present and future make up the fabric of our lives.

The Childhood Bereavement Network (CBN 2017) interviewed many young people about their experience of bereavement, and asked them to reflect on what they would advise their younger self with the benefit of hindsight. Rebekah was 15 when her mum died of cancer. She said:

> Don't worry about the people around you and don't feel that you need to be normal too soon. This could mean that grief manifests itself in unhealthy ways – accept that for the time being. Give yourself space and time... When you lose someone they don't stop being a part of who you are... I have learned that to honour my mum's memory, I must live my life to the fullest whilst I still have a heart that beats and lungs that breathe. (CBN 2017)

Many children and young people emphasise the fact that you are not on your own, although it may feel like it at the time of the bereavement. When Germaine was 15, his father died. He said:

> When my dad died it was the worst thing that had ever happened to me, but it is part of what makes me who I am today. More importantly, it's only through his death that I came to be able to help others in the same situation. It makes me happy to do so. (CBN 2017)

One area that worries those who care for and work with children and young people who are bereaved is the strength of their emotions when they experience loss. Also, they do not want 'to make things worse' for the children and young people. Well, when you think about it, can you really make matters worse when the worst has already happened?

> We are healed of a suffering only by experiencing it to the full. (Marcel Proust 2005)

Wherever possible we need to help children recognise that after the death of someone important to us we will probably revisit our relationship throughout our lives (Valentine 2008). As Julia Samuel points out (2017), dealing with bereavement is not forgetting and carrying on, but about rebuilding trust in life.

So, how can we help children and young people to love and care for themselves when someone they love has died? For the next part of this chapter, I address children and young people directly. You can adapt the sections appropriately when working with bereaved children. You could also adapt them into hand-outs or booklets that you could give to them if you think that would help.

This section speaks directly to children and young people

Love is not just a feeling but also an attitude, a way of relating to yourself as well as to others; it's a way of being in your world and involves listening to yourself as well as to others. When someone you love has died, as Phillip Ariès says, in his work on Western attitudes towards death, 'A single person is missing for you, and the whole world is empty' (Ariès 1974, as quoted in Didion 2005, p.192). Your world may seem so desperately empty, but the memories you have can never be taken away from you. Emily Dickinson wrote a poem, 'Unable Are the Loved to Die', with the following words:

> Unable are the Loved to die
> For Love is Immortality.

Living with the death of someone you love is a continual process; it lasts as long as you do. At significant points in your life memories come into sharp relief as you wish, once again, that your loved person could be with you at that important time.

Receiving the love of others

> *The supreme happiness in life is the conviction that we are loved.*

> Victor Hugo (1862)

Bereavement may bring changes that were completely unanticipated. Abigail Fuller's daughter Scout died and she felt that her heart was broken. Yet, despite the intense pain she felt, she said, 'When your heart breaks, it breaks open', and that allowed Abigail to experience 'the greatest love and gratitude I have ever known' (2009, p.4). She learned to cherish every moment she had shared with her daughter, and focused on the joy and grace they had had together rather than focusing on her loss.

When you have experienced a bereavement you may experience all sorts of feelings which may include sadness, guilt, anger, relief, emotional flatness, fear, anxiety, shame, physical pain or tiredness. Those feelings are there to facilitate recovery. They give you information about yourself and what is significant in your life. There is no 'right' way to grieve – everyone grieves in their own unique way – but it is important to realise that such feelings are normal human emotions that happen when we have had such a stressful experience. These differing feelings show you share your humanity with others who have grieved since time began.

Do small things with great love. (Mother Theresa)

It can be really helpful to share your memories with others, perhaps by looking at photographs together or recalling the best days you had together. Talk about this important person in everyday conversation, like Jane, who regularly said, 'My mum would have loved this', or her friend Kathy, 'Your Mum loved pizzas like these.'

Dr David Servan-Schrieber, a founder of the American charity Doctors Without Borders, which helps victims of war throughout the world, pledged his life to helping others. Sadly, he found he had terminal cancer at an early age and died leaving his three children to grow up without him. When he was approaching death, he wrote:

> I know that my grandparents and my father continue to live in me. It's a well-known psychological truth: when we lose someone close to us, a person whom we've loved, something of what they have bestowed on us continues to live within us and inspire us. Our dead live in our hearts. It's the most comforting form of immortality, and the one that means the most to me. (Servan-Schreiber 2011, p.133)

Your friends might give you lots of support and it can be a relief to talk to your friends when you are feeling low. In fact, they might be your first source of support. One teenager found that sending a 'grief selfie' with the text, 'Missing Mum today. She would have been 48. Happy Birthday Mum', meant that her friends knew what was going on for her without her having to talk to them. It also helped her stay connected to her mum.

In his moving account of his days with his former university lecturer who was dying, Albom quotes Morrie Schwartz: 'The most important thing in life is to learn how to give out love, and to let it come in' (2002, p.2). If you are a grieving or bereaved young person it is really important to love yourself even though might seem hard to do, and let others play a significant part as you heal from the hurt of loss.

Looking after your body

As the writer C.S. Lewis observed, 'no one ever told me that grief feels so much like fear. I am not afraid, but the sensation is like being afraid. The same flutters in the stomach, the same restlessness, the yawning. I keep on swallowing' (1961, p.5).

After someone you love dies, you may feel physically and mentally exhausted. The time leading up to the death may have been very demanding, and afterwards you can be tired out because grieving is such hard work. Caring for your physical self and personal needs plays a significant part in building your wellbeing back after the painful blow of bereavement. How can you help yourself heal, both emotionally and physically?

After bereavement, your immune system may not be functioning as strongly as it was before the death, and so you may be more susceptible to illnesses; however, you can maximise your natural defences by taking care of yourself physically and emotionally. You may find that your appetite and eating pattern change. Maybe you lose your appetite and don't feel like eating. The opposite may happen and you may eat more as a way of compensating for your loss – you may eat to fill the emptiness of grief.

Following a bereavement you can have physical symptoms such as a hollow feeling in your stomach, aching muscles, your chest may feel tight and you might have to breathe more deeply to get your breath. Sometimes, after a loved person dies, you may feel you have the same symptoms as the person who died, or you may fear that you will get the same illness. Someone this happened to was James:

> James was 16 when his father died of a brain tumour after a short illness. He seemed to be coping quite well but six months after the death he started to feel sick and having bad headaches. These are the symptoms his dad had before he was diagnosed. James was reassured by his doctor that there was no physical reason behind his symptoms, but he only started to improve when he was helped to understand the extent of his grief. (Quoted in Winston's Wish 2013, p.4)

Psychosomatic illness is an illness that is just as painful as that caused by physical causes; however, as with James, the root of the illness is in psychological distress. If you have ongoing physical symptoms, see your doctor to get a diagnosis, and if no physical cause is found, bereavement counselling could really help.

Physical activities such as running, walking or going to the gym or playing sport can all give a respite from grieving. It can also give an outlet for anger in a healthy way.

As exercise taxes your body, it releases endorphins, those feel-good factor chemicals that help you feel better, and physical activity keeps you fit. Runners, for example, say it helps their mental health, keeps them calm and brings them a sense of wellbeing. Many see it as a form of mindfulness meditation as they focus on the here and now. Physical exercise will also help you sleep. Choose activities that soothe you too.

Try to manage your energy. Pace yourself so that you don't tire yourself out. When you need to rest, accept that it is fine to do exactly that. Only undertake what you feel you can manage; don't undertake things that might be too much, especially in the early part of your bereavement. Be realistic about what you can do in physical activities, in tasks that you set yourself, and in what you say you will do for others. Be realistic about what you can do.

Looking after your emotions

Some young people who have been bereaved feel that their 'bubble has burst'. The natural joy of living, having fun, getting on with your life with your friends, that carefree state is suddenly changed. You grieve for yourself as well as for the loved one who has died. This is completely understandable and completely normal.

You may feel sad and want to cry, but you may feel that you can't cry, especially if you are a boy and have been told 'big boys don't cry'. Boys and girls grieve differently, but each does grieve. Boys may want more physical activity, getting out of the house rather than talking about the death or their feelings. Girls tend to want to talk more about their feelings such as anxiety and depression. Being 'strong' may repress feelings that will come out sometime in the future.

When grieving our emotions can change in an instant: one minute we are feeling okay and the next we are consumed by sorrow. This is par for the course. When Mark Lemon was 12, his father was stabbed to death. He said:

> The grieving process is strange. No matter how you experience it, one day you are fine and the next the grief hits you like a sledgehammer… Throughout my teenage years, my grief had turned to anger and frustration – why had this happened to me? The last thing on my mind was leaving school with good grades. But I was extremely fortunate to have a support network that kept me on the right path. (Lemon 2017)

Accept yourself

You don't have to be perfect; indeed, I have never met a perfect human being. You are a person with talents, skills and the ability to love and to be loved. Sometimes you will feel inadequate, but that is part of being human too. You may feel very distressed, which is part of the grieving process, and remember, you don't have to be strong for others. You don't have to wear a mask that says everything is fine. Give yourself permission to not be okay, if that is how you feel.

Picture yourself as the person you would like to be, picture yourself visually and in detail, and that will increase your potential to achieve it. Remember, it is the person you want to be, not what you believe other people want you to be. Your life is something you create, to be your best self. To do this you first need imagination to imagine who you want to be. You also need common sense – it's no use wanting to be a famous musician if you don't like music and have no musical talent. And you need courage, the courage to hope and to carry on through any adversity that may come your way. Have the courage to believe in yourself and the kindness to care for yourself.

Try not to ruminate

Try not to go over distressing events again and again, and try to avoid focusing on anything that makes you anxious. These emotions will come to you, but you can practise letting them go, giving yourself a break. As this ancient Chinese proverb says, you still have some control about what goes on in your head:

> You cannot prevent the birds of sorrow flying over your head, but you can prevent them from building nests in your hair.

Talking with people who are not so close to you can be helpful. Perhaps you could talk to a teacher, your form tutor, friends or a school counsellor.

Keep connected

Try not to close down your feelings as a way of coping. Sometimes we have been so hurt and shocked by what has happened that we put up barriers to keep people at a distance. This may seem to work in the short term, but it leads to isolation, and research shows that people who are isolated have more long-term complicated grief. Blocking the pain of your grief will ultimately not help, but accepting the love and support of your family and friends will be so much more beneficial. Grieving is a hard, tiring process, and where you have support it will be easier to bear.

Some bereaved young people find comfort and connection in carrying on activities that their loved one enjoyed. Daniel Tse's older brother Jason committed suicide. After the awful shock and grief, he eventually discovered that the interest they shared most, music, could help him feel motivated and cheerful. His advice to anyone grieving is to do whatever you are talented at, maybe not singing and playing guitar as for Daniel, but whatever it is, dedicate it to your loved one (CBUK 2017).

Sleeping

If you are stressed this may impact on your sleep – you may find it difficult to go to sleep or wake up earlier than you want to. Some bereaved young people have disturbing dreams or nightmares that make them anxious about going to sleep.

Establishing a routine at bedtime can help. Things that are conducive to a good sleeping pattern are to go to bed at the same time each night, have a bath, keep the light low in your bedroom and try to avoid caffeine and electronic devices in the hour before you go to bed. The aim is to have a calm hour before you settle down, to reduce stimulation and create a peaceful atmosphere.

In an article about people who have lived to be over 100 years old, Emine Saner, a journalist, discovered that gratitude played an important role in longevity and happiness. As 101-year-old Joan said, 'When I go to bed, I look back on my day and think, what was the nicest thing that happened to me today? It might be something I've seen, or something someone said, or something that I've accomplished. That's become a habit now' (quoted in Saner 2017a). It's a habit that research indicates improves wellbeing, mentally and physically.

Hope is central to this. Try to cultivate a hopeful outlook because a positive state of mind helps you to live well and to heal. Optimism is a factor here too. Concentrate on what is going well, however small this may be. Think about any positive conversations you have had, any warm feelings or anything that has given pleasure to you or to those you love.

Gratitude is such a beautiful emotion: to be grateful for things that happen in your life and the people who share your life is such a powerful experience. If you cultivate your feelings of gratitude it enriches your life in profound ways. You could try keeping a gratitude notebook. At the end of each day write down three things you are grateful for. However small the incident, if it made a positive difference to your day, record it. Doing this creates positive feelings that reduce stress levels and improve your wellbeing. It could be something you ate that tasted good, a piece of music you listened to, a butterfly in the garden, a dog wagging its tale joyfully or a funny event you witnessed. In being grateful for even the tiniest of things we increase the love in our hearts. In loving yourself when someone is dying or has died we honour those loved ones. Cherish your precious moments.

Mindfulness

Results from research into mindfulness are very impressive. If you find a quiet, calm, physical space, often in nature, it can help quell inner storms. Jon Kabat-Zinn, founder of mindfulness-based stress reduction, introduced mindfulness into hospitals in the US as an aid to recovery after surgery and in the treatment of many illnesses (1990). It has been found to have a powerful effect on building back health in recovery, and additionally it improves the immune system.

When you practise mindfulness you focus on yourself and on your breathing. As you breathe, the purpose is to be aware of your thoughts passing. You might imagine your mind as a clear blue sky and occasionally a cloud drifts across. The cloud can be seen as a thought. Let the clouds, your thoughts, continue to pass across as you breathe in and out, concentrating only on your breath; don't focus on your thoughts. This helps to bring about a restful state where you feel at peace with yourself. Try it for 15 minutes a day and see if it brings calmness and peace of mind, even if it is only for those 15 minutes.

Some people say they are too busy to do mindfulness meditation, that they have no energy or that there is too much going on in their lives. Maybe you think that too. However, as

Kabat-Zinn says, 'The more problems you have, the more you need to meditate. The more complicated your life is, the more you need to meditate – to help manage the problems and complications' (quoted in Servan-Schreiber 2011, p.83).

Emotional self-care

Focus on your inner resources and recognise that your resilience can be enhanced; you can do a lot of things to make yourself feel stronger. Knowing your own strengths and weaknesses will help you to manage your loss and grow your confidence.

Sense of competence

It's okay to have fun. Your feelings of self-worth are important in helping you build resilience and in coping with loss. Believing in your own value and worth is part of this because everyone's life matters. Listen when people praise you and comment on what they like or love about you. Take it into your heart and let your self-belief grow.

According to Professor Martin Seligman (2011), there are three kinds of happiness. First, there is the pleasant life, second, there is the good life and third, there is the meaningful life. Finding a meaningful life brings most happiness. It comes from finding something you believe in then putting your strengths to its service. It comes from having deep friendships and a wide social circle. A sense of wellbeing comes from knowing your strengths and using them.

What activities made you happy in the past? Often when we are grieving or feeling low, we stop doing those things that made us feel good in the past. We might stop seeing friends, stop hobbies that gave us pleasure or avoid places that brought joy. If you can, try to re-engage with these and allow yourself the happiness that they can bring. You are not letting your loved one down by feeling happy.

Take on new activities. These will give you completely new experiences that are not connected with your life before the person you were close to died. Creativity is important to everyone's emotional wellbeing. Try to approach things in new ways, and look at situations with fresh eyes or from different angles. Give things a go even if you have a few setbacks; this is a part of living and learning. Persevere and keep going – things often change for the better when you least expect it. Research shows that people who are happy live longer and have a wider social circle that supports them in difficult circumstances.

The comfort of small things

There is something particularly comforting about candles. Despite their fragile, flickering light that might go out at any minute, they bring light in times of darkness, when we might be feeling low. Made of natural beeswax and wicks they connect us to nature and to all our ancient ancestors who brought light into their caves to dispel the darkness and to increase feelings of safety: out of the darkness, paths of illumination can appear. Only light the candle of hope.

Music can bring a great deal of comfort in times of stress. Let the music you love help you in your grief. Maybe your favourite music will make you cry, or particular lyrics may touch your heart. If you find some quiet private space, let yourself sink into the music and allow yourself to express pent-up emotions. Make a playlist of the music your loved one enjoyed. Playing this will give you an opportunity to reconnect. You could sometimes play music to help lift your mood. Energetic music could get you dancing and dissipate some of your anxiety, and make you smile.

Aromatherapy can be very soothing and relaxing and help decrease your stress levels. Choose different oils that help with unsettling or sad moods and physical tension. Apply oils or aroma perfumes to a sweatband, scarves or in your bath. You could search online for the various properties that each plant-derived aroma comes from. Chamomile, for example, has long been known to have a calming and relaxing effect, while Frankincense is used in American and European hospitals to relieve stress and despair. Always ensure you talk to a trained therapist or your doctor before using aromatherapy products.

Making your life meaningful for you

Much of our grief can bring spiritual experiences in which you feel part of a larger world or a connection to the universal, in which all people in the natural world are connected. Sometimes as you sit in a quiet space you may sense your place in the world and an undying connection to the person who has died. You may feel yourself totally absorbed and at one with your surroundings.

Supportive social groups

A support circle, the people around you who help and care for you, has been shown to make a very positive contribution as you grieve. Your family, friends, school staff and the wider community can all help you through your time of transition following the death of someone close to you.

There are groups that offer support to bereaved children and young people, such as Winston's Wish and Child Bereavement UK. If your loved one has been in a hospice, the staff there not only look after the person with a life-limiting illness, but also care for friends and family. Ask an adult if you can go along and see what is on offer. It really can help when you discover that you are not alone, but that other people around your age have had a similar experience. It can be consoling to know that others have come through similar situations to your own.

Keeping to your normal routine is helpful, although at times you might be angry or frustrated when the adults in your life impose boundaries that seem unfair. Remember – they are probably trying to ensure you have as settled a life as possible after the upheaval you have been through. If you don't understand why routines are being maintained, ask them about their reasons.

Avoid being isolated. Some young people find it difficult to go to bed or sleep because they do not want to be alone. If that is the case for you, then talk to the people you live with and ask for their help. Maybe you could leave your bedroom door ajar so you can hear the noises in the house that will reassure you that you are not alone. Maybe you could leave a lamp on if that helps, or play some calming music or story tapes to help you drift off to sleep.

Kaey, aged 15, a boy whose beloved grandmother died and who had a lot of thoughts as he came to terms with her death, has some tips for bereaved young children:

- Find distractions.

- Cherish the memory of the person who has died.

- Go forward – don't pull back too much from others.

- Be aware that first times are very confrontational; first times can be difficult to manage, that is, when you meet friends whom you have not met since the death of your loved one.

- Do things you like: take time off from grieving.

- Sometimes it can be helpful to your friends if you tell them that you need them.

- Give yourself space and time if you need it (Westerink and Stroebe 2013).

Some children experience 'magical thinking' – they feel responsible for everything that happens in their lives. Although magical thinking is not logical, young children see themselves as the centre of their world and believe they cause things to happen. Some believe the dead will come back. This happens to adults, too, as Joan Didion describes in her brilliant book, *The Year of Magical Thinking* (2005). Although she witnessed her husband's death, she still kept his clothes and shoes because he would need them when he came back. A mother talks of her four-year-old daughter when they buried their deceased dog. While in the garden where a grave had been dug, her daughter said, 'This is really not so sad. Next spring when your tulips come up, he'll come up again and play with me' (quoted in Kübler-Ross 1985, p.83).

'Magical components are still part of [children's] thinking; they may assume that the dead person can see or hear the living, and they may work hard to please the deceased as a consequence of this' (Dyregrov 2008, p.19). We recognise magical thinking in some rituals children pursue in daily life, for example, not stepping on cracks or walking under stepladders to avoid whatever imagined catastrophe awaits them. You may believe that you are in some way responsible for your parent's illness or that, because once in heated outburst you said, 'I wish you were dead', you have brought on this situation. Try to accept that the illness or the accident has caused the death, not your thoughts, words or actions. You are not responsible for the death.

Chapter 6

MAKING MEMORIES TOGETHER WHEN SOMEONE YOU LOVE IS DYING

Let us deprive death of its strangeness.

Michel de Montaigne (quoted in Fairfield 1915, p.103)

We need to be open and honest with children and young people when someone close is ill and facing death. If we don't talk about such an important event it may lead the child to feel confused and uncertain. They may imagine more frightening scenarios, or develop misunderstandings that can be very upsetting. Not talking about an important event also gives the message that we can't cope with it, that we, the adults, can't manage the situation. We can reassure children by the way in which we talk about what is happening – our tone of voice, the words we choose, the setting we talk in and the people we include. While we recognise the sadness and intensity of the situation, if we can remain as calm as possible and be reassuring about the child's future, he will usually be able to face the pain of his present situation. Children need to feel safe in the care of those who will still be there after the ill person has died. Adults can act as models in their response to grief, which will give the child a template of how to respond in the face of grief.

The language we use is important. Militaristic language may teach the child the idea that he, too, has to fight. For example, talking about cancer, such as battling the illness, fighting the enemy and so on, as seen on cancer charity publicity campaigns, does not allow for the reality of the person who has the illness and those around him. They may feel inadequate because they haven't got the energy for the 'war on illness'. In her book *Thrive*, Arianna Huffington points out that talking about death is still a taboo for many, yet, she asks, 'Where are our culture's preparations for leaving life with gratitude and grace?' (2014, p.201). How can we help children and young people incorporate gratitude and grace in their lives to celebrate the life of their loved one who is facing death?

In all religions, death has a central role, and most philosophies are concerned with it too. In Plato's *Phaedo*, Socrates states, 'The one aim of those who practice philosophy in the proper manner is to practice for death and dying' (quoted in Donnelly 1994, p.1). The ancient Romans gave us the term 'memento mori', which means remember death, remember that we are all mortal and we will all die. In thinking about death, we can consider how best to live our lives and what we want to contribute to the lives of others and to the world we live in. Elisabeth Kübler-Ross, in her book *Death: The Final Stage of Growth* (1975), said that for her, working with people who were dying was not morbid but life-enhancing. She called death 'a highly creative force...facing death means facing the ultimate question of the meaning of life. If we really want to live we must have the courage to recognize that life is ultimately very short and that everything we do counts' (1975, p.1). In the end, it is not money or power that defines a 'good death', but doing the simple things that count, simple things like telling family and friends that you love them, expressing gratitude for acts of kindness, appreciating the beauty of nature and valuing the gifts in your life.

We may be able to help young people who are living with someone who is dying to develop skills of gratitude and grace, to accept the gifts that this precious time gives them, to 'be here now', to be in the moment, to be present and to try not to fear what we don't know. Leading palliative care physician Dr Ira Bycock wrote in *Dying Well: The Prospect for Growth at the End of Life* (1997), that conversations at this point in life can bring profound healing and connection despite the suffering and sadness that may also be there. Where relationships have been fraught, there is the opportunity to mend and nurture the relationships, particularly with adolescents. In a lecture Bycock gave to the Victoria Palliative Care team in Australia in 2013, 'Saying the Four Things that Matter Most for Living and Dying Well', he talked of 'Saying please forgive me', 'I forgive you', 'I love you' and saying 'Thank you' (Bycock 2014). Following his example, we could encourage young people to have a conversation if it seems appropriate. Well-chosen words can bring emotional wellbeing and strength to families with a terminally ill member, and celebrate the relationship they have had together (Yalom 2011).

In the book *A Monster Calls* by Patrick Ness (2011), the boy in the story, Connor, struggles because no one tells him the truth about his sick mother. He knows that something serious is happening but no one tells him she is dying. This exclusion creates a situation in which the 'monster' comes to bring him painful truths. The monster embodies Connor's darkest secret, that he wants his mother to die. He cannot bear to watch his mother as she is dying, and he wants her suffering to end. This is a secret that other young people in real, living situations may share but never speak of. It is a very powerful story that reveals how by not having truthful conversations we disempower children, and may even create serious problems for them.

Even when the person has a diagnosis of terminal illness, they are never prepared for death because, not having experienced it before, how can they know what will happen? Exploring the fears that lurk and trying to meet the needs of the person and his family can help. Also, encouraging people to try not to have any regrets about not saying or doing the things they really want to say or do.

ANTICIPATORY GRIEF

Anticipatory grief occurs prior to a loss rather than the grief that comes after a loss (bereavement grief). As lives are prolonged because of advances in medical treatment, for example, in the cases of some cancers, or lives are protracted by palliative care, anticipatory grief is more common, and the patient and family experience a great deal of stress and feelings of vulnerability. While care is being given to the dying person, it arouses an intense range of emotions in the patient and those who share his life. These experiences are termed 'anticipatory grief reactions'. They begin with diagnosis and end with death when bereavement grief takes over. Wherever possible, help the child or young person to pace himself so he can absorb painful information. It can be extremely difficult to think about all the things that go with end of life. Truth told in small amounts over several days or weeks gives the child the chance to adjust to what he can understand while he is still carrying on with his own routines and activities (Bylund-Grenko *et al.* 2014).

After a devastating diagnosis that there is no further treatment available to cure the patient, all the family are in pain. For the sick person, his suffering is shared by those closest to him, even when this is not spoken of. In fact, suffering in silence may be the hardest thing – when nobody wants to speak the truth or is unable or is not allowed to speak, each person is isolated in their grief. We also need to bear in mind that it takes courage to have conversations that matter about the end of life.

In her booklet, *Good Grief: What Will We Tell the Kids?*, Ana Draper talks of the importance of good communication when a child's parent or sibling is dying:

> studies show that good communication really helps the grieving process – and a good process before someone dies can really help a child to re-establish their life and to re-imagine their future without their loved one – without their loved one, yes, but a positive nevertheless, in which the memory of, and connection with the person they've lost helps them to live their own lives as fully as they can. (Draper 2008, p.2)

Anticipatory grief gives the dying person the opportunity to prepare for death and to make adjustments in his present and future. On a practical level this may involve making a will, finishing 'unfinished business' or leaving final messages. Spiritual care may also be offered or requested by both the dying person and his family and friends. The emotional intensity of anticipatory grief may increase in intensity as death comes closer.

Uncertainty is one of the striking features of anticipatory grief. As 14-year-old Gemma says, 'until it ends you just don't know...' (quoted in Chowns 2013, p.20). Children and young people notice changes in their parent's behaviour and physical changes that may be disturbing. Medication may also influence the ability for patients to be present. Physically they are there but they may be unavailable because morphine, for example, may bring drowsiness and absence. This can be confusing and disheartening for young people. On the positive side it may lead to the child becoming more independent and personally resourceful because he cannot fully rely on the parent as he had done previously before serious illness entered his life.

In palliative care, truthfulness is absolutely crucial. However, parents may withhold information in the hope that the sick person will get better, which means they may not communicate honestly (Barnes *et al.* 2000; Chowns 2013). Children in the family may also feel marginalised, that everyone else knows what is going on but that they are excluded from the inner circle of those who do know. Children want information so they can be supportive to their parents and family. Children and young people with a seriously ill family member want to make active contributions, to feel part of the ongoing situation and be empowered to step up to the demands such a situation brings. As Chowns concludes:

> we need to critically examine our taken-for-granted assumptions about childhood and vulnerability and move towards a better understanding of children in contemporary society – one that acknowledges not only the needs of young people but also their capacity and competence to deal with

the challenges of living with serious illness and anticipated parental death. (Chowns 2013, p.30)

In end-of-life care, a holistic assessment of the needs of the patient should include the spiritual dimension as well as physical, social and psychological needs. In terms of spirituality, the faith of the person, his religious and non-religious beliefs and values, life, personal or future goals, as well as his worries and challenges about his illness and how this impacts on his faith or beliefs, these all need to be taken into account. In assessing the needs of the patient, those who care for him will also need to consider how to include the family and the children who are part of it. Improving the quality of care of the person at the end of life will very likely improve the lives of those closest to him.

When children are sad, in emotional pain or angry, they give off signals to others to stay away when what they really want and need is to be loved. This is especially the case when they are fearful about losing a parent. Research has shown that children whose parent is dying have 'an instinctive drive to survive, and so move towards the living parent and away from their dying one' (Samuel 2017, p.98). It is important to encourage them to keep their relationship with their dying parent and enable them to be involved in their care in whatever feels possible for the child, as this will be important following the death and throughout later milestones in their ongoing life.

Children whose sibling is facing death have similar anxieties to those whose parent is dying. Eleven-year-old Gary knew his seven-year-old sister had only a short time, and wrote about his feelings:

> I felt sad in my heart. Fear was a lump in my throat.
>
> In my head I felt guilty, I thought it was my fault. I was so angry, the anger was coming out of my head, my eyes, everywhere. (Hitcham 1995, quoted in Smith and Pennells 1995, p.35)

Accepting death, our own or that of our loved one, is an intense, emotional challenge. Often we fear that the emotions will overwhelm or destroy, that they will never end; however, when we open ourselves to the reality of grief work, we can discover hidden depths and aspects of ourselves. As Julie Brams-Prudeaux, a licensed marriage and family therapist and eco-psychologist, says, 'Grief work provides us with the chance to deepen ourselves, to define who we are, and to live out a meaningful and purposeful life' (Brams-Prudeaux 2005, p.2).

In *Not the Last Goodbye: Reflections on Life, Death, Healing and Cancer* (2011), Dr David Servan-Schreiber writes about his own cancer, his life and treatment and, finally, his approaching death. Of his patients, he wrote, 'I believe that most of them saw death as a transition, a passage from the life we know to something else we cannot know. A transition similar to birth, but going the other way' (2011, p.98).

The founder of the hospice movement, Dame Cicely Saunders, believed that, 'The window of suffering can be a window to peace and opportunity' (quoted in Ferrell and Coyle 2001). In the midst of tremendous suffering, she recognised that there are moments of beauty and possibility. For her original research she recorded over 1000 patient stories. She connected with the narratives of their lives and used them to underpin therapeutic treatment in end-of-life care (Mallon 2009).

At the end of life, doctors cannot always cure, but they can connect and make a positive contribution to those they care for. Connections and conversations that are meaningful may lead to heightened emotions, but tears and sadness are normal at such a poignant, intense time. These conversations will not have all the answers the child wants because even the doctors in control of diagnosis and treatment do not know all the answers. They don't know of the twists and turns that the disease may take, and children will accept that. Where there is honesty, children will trust as they realise you will tell them the truth, even when it is really hard (Dougy Center 2017).

In some cases the people who live on after the death may feel 'survivor guilt', particularly if the death seems out of the natural order. A father may feel survivor guilt if his young son dies, and there may be the unspoken idea, 'Why him and not me? I should have been the one to die.'

Julia Samuel, in her book *Grief Works*, emphasises that dealing with bereavement is not about forgetting and moving on, but about rebuilding trust in life. As we once more learn to trust we can re-invest in our own futures.

Children sense change, they notice physical changes in the sick person and may notice that more friends and relatives are visiting or helping out, so it is better for adults to share their knowledge. The person who has a life-limiting illness may struggle with intense feelings. One woman whose husband died of cancer, Pieta, says:

> It was his way of dealing with his cancer. He was very angry. He didn't want anyone to know, not his friends, his family or the children, who were six and nine at the time. For me this is not the way I function. I found ways of talking with the children about illness and death at bedtime, in story terms, answering their questions when they felt ready to ask. (Quoted in Petrone 1999, p.24)

In June 2000, I attended a workshop led by the artist Michele Angelo Petrone. He spoke about his cancer journey and how his art had allowed him to express his fears about illness and death. Aged 30, he was diagnosed with Hodgkin's lymphoma and in his isolated hospital room he used his talent to express complex feelings about the physical effects, the assaults of his treatment and his fear of dying. He said, 'I need to know that this body is my body. And I need to know everything that is happening to my body. But most of all I need to know that you know that within my body there is me' (Buchan 2007). Like so many who face crippling illness and death, he still wanted to be recognised as a unique human being, someone who was more than the sum of his symptoms and treatment.

Michele ran hundreds of workshops showing how painting can help those with life-limiting illness and for the healthcare professionals who care for them. Through art they could express emotions that were too difficult to express verbally.

He said, 'Nothing had prepared me for what I was about to go through… It was more difficult and painful than I had ever imagined. But part of that pain and difficulty came out of fear and ignorance. My fear and the fear of everyone around me' (quoted in Buchan 2007). People can find meaning, peace and resolution through their paintings, as Petrone demonstrated. He died in 2007, aged 43, having written *The Emotional Cancer Journey* (2003).

Perhaps we can encourage young people to let go of what they can't control and to cherish what they have. To understand they cannot control the illness of someone they love, but they can live every moment they have in the present, now. The essential aspect of this highly emotional time is that the family communicate about what is happening, and take it day by day, enjoying the life that is left to them (Moore 2009). If the family can talk to each other about difficult issues before death, communication will be easier in the future.

When someone is dying, it is likely that the child or young person feels there is no anchor to keep him safe because everything is changing, day to day, and in some instances, hour to hour. It may be that the child needs special support before his loved one dies. Hospices offer pre-bereavement care to help patients and families in the run-up to the end of life. Children's stress levels may increase dramatically at this time because of their fears and anxiety about the unknown future. Pre-bereavement counselling offers the child the opportunity to talk about his feelings and to share his worries, which brings both clarity and comfort.

In a way, when someone is dying the whole family is the patient because everyone will be experiencing some form of loss. Bereavement begins on the day of diagnosis, as the patient and the family fear the changes that will come. The changing roles and relationships often alter in a way that is not wanted. Isolation and feeling alone may start within the family. For the young person whose loved one is dying, it is important to find ways of taking the person with him, not letting go, but taking the best he can of the relationship and sealing it in his heart. Steve Hewlett, a British broadcaster who died from oesophageal cancer in 2017, and who described his illness and feelings to BBC Radio 4 presenter, Eddie Mair, wrote, 'I'm absolutely convinced that the more we talk about cancer – both to our families, friends and loved ones – the better it is for all concerned. Above all it is empowering for them.'[1]

We cannot shield children from painful events that are part of our living existence. If we lie to children or exclude them from the illness or impending death of someone close to them, we may deprive them of the opportunity to make important contributions to that relationship. However, this is not an easy task for family or for professionals involved in the care of a terminally ill person and his family (Macpherson 2017). There may be tensions around respect for the needs of the dying person, concern about cultural values and differences, and meeting the child's needs without undermining family relationships.

When someone we love is dying we have to live with a reality that we wish wasn't true. We live in a culture that seems to say that everything can be fixed but the reality is far from the truth. As grief psychotherapist Julia Samuel says, 'Grief is the antithesis of this belief: it eschews avoidance and requires endurance, and forces us to accept that there are some things in this world that simply cannot be fixed' (quoted in Kellaway 2017).

Children are entitled to receive answers to their questions and to be given information that clearly explains what has happened and is happening and what will happen next (Cranwell 2007). Of course, there may not be definite answers about an unknown future, but by explaining that the child will be protected, loved and cared for, a great deal of fear may be alleviated. The circumstances cannot be changed, but you can help children develop a more positive hope for their future. As poet Diane Hedges says in *Poetry, Therapy, and Emotional Life* (2015, p.141), writing on loss, 'Hope is often a feeling that

---

1   See www.radiotimes.com/news/2016-10-11/bbc-radio-4-broadcaster
     -steve-hewlett-telling-my-boys-about-my-cancer-was-the-hardest-
     thing-ive-ever-had-to-do

is completely missing when losses occur. Hope is the sense of possibility...the sense of a way out and a destiny that goes somewhere, even if not to the specific place one had in mind.' We can assist by helping children imagine a more positive state in the future and to recover a positive sense of themselves.

Final conversations can be treasured in the future. As Cranwell (2007, p.31) said of Sophie, one of the young people who took part in his research with children whose parent had died, 'She recalled her mother dying saying to her, "You're my beautiful girl and I'm so proud of you." Then her mother said, "We'll meet again."'

It can be comforting for children to develop rituals, such as:

- Lighting a candle or listening to special music.

- Organising a special place for thinking privately, or for writing or drawing.

- Drawing on any religious or spiritual beliefs, if this is helpful.

- Doing things that are soothing such as being in nature or meditation.

- Thinking about customs or rituals that are meaningful and creating mental and physical space to engage with them.

NARRATIVE MEDICINE

Narrative medicine facilitates the expression of feelings and thoughts. Andrew Solomon, a journalist, wrote, 'The emerging field of narrative medicine proposes that patients can be treated correctly only when they can tell the story of their illness, often in the context of a more extensive autobiography' (2016, p.2).

Medicine in its central core is about the human endeavour. It's not just about the technology, the drugs, the advances in surgery – all of which are supremely important – but the heart of treatment is about relationship and the listening to and the telling of stories. In building continuing bonds with children, all these stories have a place, wherever possible. The child should be asked how much he wants to be involved with decision-making and in the ongoing care of the terminally ill person as he goes through this period of transition.

In many ways, those who are ill and those who care for them have stories to tell, not only about the illness, but also about the lives that are impacted by the illness. The dead 'live on' in the memories of those who survive them (Parkes 1988). A person is embedded inside the ill body, and embedded in those who witness the changes in the sick person and who themselves are changed by it.

'In examining disease, we gain wisdom about anatomy and physiology and biology. In examining the person with disease, we gain wisdom about life' (Sacks 1985, p.3). We need to be open and aware of how adults, children and young people experience the death of someone they love. It is an eye-opening experience that we would like to close our eyes to. Oliver Sacks also said, 'Language, that most human invention, can enable what, in principle, should not be possible. It can allow all of us, even the congenitally blind, to see with another person's eyes' (Sacks 2010, p.240).

Facing a terminal diagnosis or facing end-of-life care brings a time of transition. The need to be creative and to live in a meaningful way is important for the patient, his family and carers. The psychological distress, physical challenges and cognitive challenges are incredibly demanding. Expressive writing and the arts in general can alleviate distress and give social support at a time when feelings of isolation exacerbate anxiety. Writing can also act as a legacy for those who share the life of the person facing the end of his life. The writing makes a story that tells of significant actions in life over a period of time. These stories are an effective way of sharing feelings, knowledge and history with others in their circle.

When initiating writing activities, the following points can aid the process:

- Try to find out what the child understands about the situation.

- What does the child understand about death? Obviously, the age of the child and level of maturity will influence his knowledge.

- What does the child feel? Feelings such as guilt, shame, fear and anxiety are not uncommon. Try to clarify what impact these feelings are having on the child, and ensure you rectify any mistaken ideas he might have picked up. Confusion can add to the child's stress.

- Children often feel that they or another member of their family will become ill. Try to reassure the child.

- Offer or get support for the child so he does not feel isolated.

In the time of transition that is bereavement, expressive writing can alleviate some of the pain and may help the young person understand the landscape he is traversing. It remains a record of where he has travelled.

An acrostic for a person's name can be revealing and provide new insights for the writer. This is a simple exercise to facilitate the expression of feelings and thoughts. Jane Moss (2012), who led a creative writing group at Princess Alice Hospice in London, recalled a moving acrostic written by Linda, a group member:

Love
Is
Never
Dying
Alone

Where a young person is facing the likely death of a parent, he will prefer support and understanding rather than protection from the truth. He will want to be told truthfully, as soon as possible. Children and young people don't want to be kept in the dark (Chowns 2013). Usually the period before an anticipated death is more stressful than after death because there is so much uncertainty (Christ 2000).

It is also important to facilitate any legacies the terminally ill person wants to pass on. Some examples I have come across are making a video for each child that says something important about their relationship, leaving letters expressing love and hopes for the children's future, and photographs for those who remain behind.

THE IMPORTANCE OF EMPATHY

Jane Moss also wrote about the importance of happiness, emphasising that people in the healthcare professions should ask patients and clients about what makes them happy (2012). In asking the question she found out what priorities the patients had, what obstacles they faced that prevented them from being happy, and worked with them to achieve their happiness goals. When we listen to those we work with and care about, we can find out about what their lives mean to them and how they want to live it.

MAKING A MEMORY BOX

Sometimes it is possible that a parent who is terminally ill can make a memory box with his child or children. They can decide together what to include that reminds them both of their time together. It gives a tangible link that will remain after the death, and can bring comfort as the child grows and develops.

DIGNITY THERAPY

Dignity therapy is an individualised, short-term therapeutic technique for patients living with life-limiting or life-threatening illness. It addresses the need that many people have to leave something of themselves behind after they die. It involves a conversation between the therapist and patient that is then recorded, transcribed and edited into a narrative that can be passed on to people the patient wishes to share it with. Dr Harvey Max Chochinov, from the University of Manitoba in Canada, pioneered the approach to help with the end-of-life experience (2003). The therapy seems to help people build a legacy to help those left behind.

LIVING WITH DYING

When they were in their teens, Felix White and his brother Hugo lived with their parents. Their mother had multiple sclerosis, which eventually left her bedridden. When they went into her room, even though she was shaking uncontrollably, she would smile at them. Felix felt that it was her way of protecting them and trying to keep happiness in their lives.

In retrospect Felix realised that her illness and death affected them more than he recognised at the time. The brothers didn't fight as siblings often do because, at a deep level, they knew that their own feelings were less important than the serious matter of their mother's illness, and they did not want to make things any more difficult for their parents than they already were.

The brothers channelled their emotions into music, as a distraction from the pain and sadness in their home. Later, they formed the hugely successful band The Maccabees, and felt sure it was the power of wanting their mother to be proud of them and their achievements that drove them on.

Like many other young people whose parent is terminally ill or who has died, Hugo cut himself off. He couldn't see how anyone outside the family could understand what was going on, and as it was, he and his three brothers and father didn't speak about the death of Hugo's mother. In retrospect he realises that they were all wrestling with profound feelings of loss, although they were still determined to create a successful career (Scott 2016).

WRITING LETTERS

Those who are living with a life-limiting illness may be very concerned about the lives of those they leave behind, particularly parents who are dying. In hospices, family support workers and counsellors can help patients to write letters to their children to be opened after death or at a predetermined time, such as a significant birthday.

Writing letters can be very cathartic. Some people go on to publish these letters, as psychotherapist Gael Lindenfield did. When her 19-year-old daughter died, she wrote letters to her, 'and it was very healing to write everything down' (quoted in Davies 2014, p.16).

MAKING LISTS

When Kate Greene was dying of breast cancer she wrote a list that left a lasting impression on her husband Singe and her sons, Reef and Finn. The list was turned into a book (2012), then a film (2016), called *Mum's List*. The list included requests such as to kiss the boys twice every night – one kiss from Singe, the other from her. She urged her husband to find a new partner, so that the boys could have a strong female influence in their lives. As the family tick off the 'bucket list' Kate left – such as seeing the Northern Lights or going to Switzerland, where Singe had proposed to her – they remember their continuing bond with their remarkable mother.

In an interview with the journalist Tanith Carey, Reef was asked what his mother wanted for him by writing the list. He replied 'happiness' (Carey 2016). For bereaved children to know this with such certainty helps the mourning process immeasurably. As Singe said:

> The things on the list are what Kate and I both wanted to do and how we both wanted to live our lives. She may be gone, but the boys get bits of their mum by doing the things she enjoyed and what she loved to do. They know her better that way... It's like leaving footprints on a beach – you walk up and the wave comes and the footprints are gone. This is a way to keep the footprints still there... (Quoted in Carey 2016)

In 'The connection between art, healing and public health: A review of current literature', researchers Heather Stuckey and Jeremy Nobel concluded, 'Use of the arts in healing does not contradict the medical view in bringing emotional, somatic, artistic and spiritual dimensions to learning. Rather, it complements the biomedical view by focusing on not only sickness and symptoms themselves but the holistic nature of the person' (2010, p.267). The holistic approach to dying and death may include lists that cover a myriad of aspects that include physical, creative and personal desires.

The poet, Emily Dickinson, said that forever is composed of nows. The challenge is to stop worrying about the future and to live in the nows that we have. This can have no greater relevance than when we are living with someone who is dying.

Chapter 7

USEFUL RESOURCES

BIBLIOTHERAPY

The Reading Well for Young People campaign was launched in England in 2016 by The Reading Agency.1 It aims to help young people who are experiencing stress or have mental health difficulties to seek comfort and support through books, fiction in particular. Young people involved are recommended 'mood-busting books' and adults, librarians and professionals offer choices that may help young people to face and understand feelings and thoughts about loss and bereavement. The list of books below includes some of the titles The Reading Agency recommends, because, as they say, 'everything changes when we read.'

Bibliotherapy involves using books to help children deal with their problems. In reading books or listening to stories children can explore their feelings about their own losses and grief. I have assembled a list that you might find useful. The ages are for guidance only – children's reading age and emotional maturity vary so widely that a young child may be more than able to appreciate books aimed at an older age group. Have a look at the books and make up your own mind based on your knowledge of the child you are working with.

I have included choices from a variety of sources that I hope will provide a rich selection for anyone involved in the

---

1 See https://readingagency.org.uk/young-people/quick-guides/reading -well

lives of bereaved and grieving children. Many of the books listed have been made into films that could be watched with children and young people.

BOOKS FOR 5- TO 8-YEAR-OLDS

The Huge Bag of Worries by Virginia Ironside, illustrated by Frank Rodgers, Hodder Children's Books, 2011

> Jenny has lots of different worries and they begin to build up and get out of control. Try as she might, she can't get rid of them until the old neighbour next door helps her feel better. A lovely story, well illustrated, which encourages children to talk about what is making them anxious. You could also make a bag to put the 'worries' in and use it with groups.

Am I Still A Sister? by Alicia M. Sims, illustrated by Jim Maus, Big A & Co., 1988

> A thoughtful book written by a young person. The 11-year-old girl's 13-month-old brother died. It addresses a whole range of emotions and situations following sibling bereavement.

Badger's Parting Gifts by Susan Varley, Andersen Press Ltd, 2013

> Badger is old and knows he will soon die. When he does, his animal friends think they will be sad forever, but then they talk about their memories of Badger and the things Badger taught them. Gradually they cope with his death and value the legacies he left them. This is a lovely picture book that emphasises the importance of remembering the one who has died. I've used this book with all ages, including adults, as it really helps explore the significance of the continuing bonds we have with those who have died.

Geranium Morning: A Book about Grief by E. Sandy Powell, illustrated by Renee Graef, Carolrhoda Books, 1990

> This book tells the story of two children, one who experiences a sudden death while the other experiences an expected death. The story shows how the children cope, how they get support from other people and strive to make sense of what has happened.

Heaven by Nicholas Allan, Red Fox Picture Books, 2014

> Dill, the dog, knows his time is up, so he packs his case and tells Lily, his owner, that he is going on his way 'Up there'. Lily asks if

she can come too but Dill says 'Not yet'. As he waits for the angels to take him to heaven they talk about what they think heaven is like. For Dill, it is full of lampposts, lots of stinky things to smell and bones to gnaw. Lily has a completely different idea of heaven. The book explores ideas about heaven and the afterlife as well as exploring how we say a last goodbye.

I'll Always Love You by Hans Wilhelm, Crown Publishers Inc., 1988

This is a moving story of a boy's love of the dog he has grown up with. He and his family mourn the dog and bury him in their garden. Although the boy is very sad, he is comforted by the fact he remembers telling his dog, 'I'll always love you' every night.

Luna's Red Hat: An Illustrated Story Book to Help Children Cope with Loss and Suicide by Emmi Smid, Jessica Kingsley Publishers, 2015

For children aged 6+, this book follows a little girl called Luna whose mother died a year before. It deals with death by suicide and how to cope with the difficult feelings that follow such a death. The book also includes a guide for parents and professionals by a grief specialist. The author says, 'The name Luna is not a coincidence. Luna is Latin for moon. Symbolically, the name Luna stands for transition, renewal and balance. I thought it a suitable and hopeful name for a young girl who is coming to terms with the death of her mother.' (The Story Behind *Luna's Red Hat* 2015)

Goodbye Mog by Judith Kerr, HarperCollins Children's Books, 2002

The much-loved cat Mog gets very old and very tired and dies, but a little bit stays around and watches the family's reactions. The family get a new kitten who is shy and nervous, and the ghost Mog helps it settle down. It is a lovely story, but when reading it to children ensure that they understand that when Mog wants to sleep forever, 'And so she did', sleep is not to be confused with death. It is a classic euphemism for death and should be avoided.

No Matter What by Debi Gliori, Bloomsbury Publishing, 1999

This tale of unconditional love features Small, a little fox, who is feeling grumpy and anxious. In rhyming text and with colourful illustrations, Small is reassured by his mother Big, who repeatedly says, 'I will always love you, no matter what.' The emphasis is that a parent's love is limitless, and this could bring much reassurance to a bereaved child who needs to feel secure.

Rafi's Red Racing Car: Explaining Suicide and Grief to Young Children by Louise Moir, Jessica Kingsley Publishers, 2016

Rafi is a rabbit who loves playing with his daddy and with his favourite toy, a red racing car. Rafi's daddy gets so sad and confused that one day, he goes out and doesn't come back. Rafi is scared and confused. This compassionate, beautifully illustrated book aims to help young children to come to terms with the loss of a family member by suicide. Rafi's story is explained in a sensitive yet honest way, and helps us to understand the overwhelming myriad emotions of grief. With love, guidance, therapeutic activities and fun memories kept alive in his red racing car, Rafi gradually begins to feel happy again, and to reinvest in life.

The Invisible String by Patrice Karst, illustrated by Geoff Stevenson, De Vorss & Co., 2000

The mother of twins Jeremy and Liza explains to them that we are all connected by an invisible string that is made of love. The story is simply told and shows how love is a powerful, unending bond that touches our hearts and keeps us connected, no matter how we are separated. It is a delightful book that would be a comfort for bereaved children, and reinforces the concept of continuing bonds.

The Tenth Good Thing about Barney by Judith Viorst, illustrated by Erik Blegvad, Aladdin Paperbacks, 1987

After a young boy's cat dies, he is sad and doesn't want to eat. His mother suggests that they will bury the cat in the garden and that Barney could think about ten good things to say at the funeral. He can only think of nine and asks his father about what happens to someone after they have died. He learns that the body of his cat will help the flowers grow. He discovers the tenth thing, the cycle of life. It is a carefully written book that sensitively deals with death and lets readers decide for themselves about what happens after the funeral.

Water Bugs and Dragonflies: Explaining Death to Children by Doris Stickney, illustrated by Gloria Ortiz Hernandez, The Pilgrim Press, 1982

This best-selling book is based on a fable linking death with the water bug's transformation into a dragonfly. It gives a sensitive and straightforward explanation about death. It deals with the mysteries about death and what happens after we die. It is based on Christian beliefs as a focus on life after death, and contains advice for parents. It introduces the idea of the life cycle. You can also get a colouring book format, too, to use with bereaved children.

When Dinosaurs Die: A Guide to Understanding Death by Laurie Krasney Brown, illustrated by Marc Brown, Little Brown Books, 1998

This well-illustrated book explores topics and questions about death including saying goodbye, and customs, rituals and beliefs about death. Religious and humanistic views are taken into account and the book provides a sound basis to open up discussions with children.

When Uncle Bob Died (Talking it Through) by Althea, illustrated by Sarah Wimperis, Dinosaur Publications, 1982

This lovely book addresses fear, anger, sadness and the memories that remain after a loved one dies. It offers a starting point for discussing death and thoughts about it.

The Velveteen Rabbit. Or, How Toys Become Real by Margery Williams, illustrated by William Nicholson, Egmont, 2017

This children's classic was first published in 1922. It is the powerful story of a little stuffed rabbit, his love for a boy and how he becomes real. When Boy contracts scarlet fever, all his toys and books have to be destroyed, but Velveteen Rabbit manages to survive and is so well loved he becomes Real. Although not focused on death, it deals with separation and the undying bonds we have through love.

James and the Giant Peach by Roald Dahl, George Allen & Unwin, 1967

James lives with his gruesome aunts following the death of his parents who were eaten by an escaped rhinoceros. One day a strange, huge peach grows in the back garden and so change begins to happen. The book shows how the spirit to survive against the odds, with the help of friends, carries James through his adventure. As in the hero's journey, James' call to adventure after the death of his parents leads him to a new life.

The BFG by Roald Dahl, illustrated by Quentin Blake, Puffin Books, 1984

Sophie's parents died when she was a baby and she is living in an orphanage when the Big Friendly Giant (BFG) snatches her away. He cries when she tells him of the cruelty of Mrs Clonkers who runs the orphanage. As their adventure progresses Sophie learns that the BFG blows lovely golden dreams into children's heads as they sleep. Dahl's glorious inventive language touches on sadness, cruelty and resilience.

What Happened to Daddy's Body? Explaining What Happens after Death in Words Very Young Children Can Understand by Elke Barber and Alex Barber, illustrated by Anna Jarvis, Jessica Kingsley Publishers, 2016

Alex wants to know what happened to his daddy's body after he died. What was the box they put him into? The book reflects age-appropriate language without the use of euphemisms, and gives the clear message that it's okay to be sad but that it's okay to be happy too.

Is Daddy Coming Back in a Minute? Explaining Sudden Death to Pre-School Children in Words They Can Understand by Elke Barber and Alex Barber, illustrated by Anna Jarvis, Jessica Kingsley Publishers, 2016

The book explains sudden death in a way that young children can understand. Based on a true event, the story shows how Alex's mum helped him to understand what 'dead' means.

Muddles, Puddles and Sunshine: Your Activity Book to Help When Someone Has Died by Diana Crossley, illustrated by Kate Sheppard, Hawthorn Press, 2000

This delightful book, mainly aimed at primary school-aged children, provides lots of material to find meaning in their loss, to explore their emotions and to build continuing bonds with the deceased through numerous memory activities. The emphasis of the book is to have fun while engaging in inexpensive, creative activities.

Seeds of Hope: Bereavement and Loss Activity Book: Helping Children and Young People Cope with Change through Nature by Caroline Jay, illustrated by Unity-Joy Dale, Jessica Kingsley Publishers, 2014

This book uses nature to understand death, loss and change in a gentle way. It has a delightful range of creative activities such as choosing an insect or plant and using it to draw a life cycle, or making a paper memory tree of happy and sad memories. The activities help the child explore, recognise and accept feelings that loss engenders.

BOOKS FOR 9- TO 12-YEAR-OLDS

Charlotte's Web by E.B. White, illustrated by Garth Williams, Puffin Classics, 2014

This story tells of the powerful relationship between a little girl called Fern, Wilber the pig, and Charlotte the spider. The story is infused with the spirit of friendship, the power of love, and the presence of death in life. It beautifully describes the life cycle and the enduring bonds of love within a compelling story.

Harry Potter Series by J.K. Rowling, Bloomsbury, 1997–2007

The bestselling Harry Potter series, also in film and video, charts Harry's hero's journey from being orphaned to overcoming adversity and finding joy in life. Death features significantly throughout the books, from his ongoing sense of the loss of his parents to the deaths of Dumbledore and Sirius. His relationship with his parents continues in his dreams, and in learning about them through the memories of others who knew them. The continuing bonds Harry has weave through these gripping books.

His Dark Materials Trilogy by Philip Pullman, Scholastic, 1995, 1997, 2000

Many children already know this award-winning trilogy. The brilliant story line covers bereavement, relationships, religion and spirituality. A fast-paced adventure propels the reader through a series of events that relate to the emotional roller coaster that is life.

The Cat Mummy by Jacqueline Wilson, illustrated by Nick Sharratt, Macmillan Children's Books, 2015

Verity's mother died the day she was born, but she rarely talks about her because she doesn't want to upset her father or grandparents. The story focuses on her cat Mabel, who goes missing, and this unfolds to reveal the misunderstandings children can have about death. It is amusing and moving and shows how important it is to be open, honest and to talk about difficult issues. The positive ending is heart-warming.

Double Act by Jacqueline Wilson, illustrated by Nick Sharratt and Sue Heap, Corgi Yearling, 2006

Ten-year-old twins, Ruby and Garnet, do everything together, especially since their mother died three years ago. When their father finds a new partner they have yet more changes, including moving house. After getting into all sorts of trouble, they eventually settle down and learn to live with the changes. This is a sensitive and funny story that addresses many types of loss.

Dustbin Baby by Jacqueline Wilson, illustrated by Nick Sharratt, Corgi, 2007

April was abandoned as a baby on 1 April. She has spent her life in a children's home and with different foster parents, one of whom committed suicide. She has had a difficult life, and on her 14th birthday she sets off to find out more about her past. This book has a great storyline – as usual with Jacqueline Wilson – and explores many issues about loss.

Vicky Angel by Jacqueline Wilson, illustrated by Nick Sharratt, Corgi Yearling, 2005

Jade's best friend Vicky dies in a tragic car accident. Jade is devastated by the loss and the story tells how she copes when Vicky appears to her as a ghost. Her life seems to unravel, and eventually Jade sees a counsellor who helps her find herself and her life path.

Michael Rosen's Sad Book by Michael Rosen, illustrated by Quentin Blake, Walker Books, 2004

This award-winning, beautifully illustrated book, explores Michael Rosen's sadness following the death of his son Eddie. It offers so much insight into the impact of bereavement, including the way we mask our true feelings. It has small snippets of text and shows how we all have sad stuff. Michael talks about how the sadness about his son's death comes and covers him, and about how he manages it, and makes you smile at his memories. This is a brilliant book that I have used with both children and adults.

Goodnight Mister Tom by Michelle Magorian, illustrated by Neil Reed, Puffin Classics, 1981

A story of love, loss, bereavement and hope, as young Willie Beech is evacuated from London as Britain is on the brink of the Second World War. An emotional and physically abused child of a mentally ill mother, Willie gradually flourishes under the care of a gruff, isolated man in his sixties in the countryside and in his friendship with a boy called Zach. This award-winning book is gripping, hard-hitting and profoundly moving. It also has a thread of continuing bonds and resilience running through the whole text. Willie's grieving is depicted so realistically, as is the way he finds the strength to carry on under the loving care of Mister Tom. In trying to think like his dead friend Zach he continues Zach's life within his own with an unbreakable bond that gives him great comfort.

Skellig by David Almond, Hodder Children's Books, 1998

A widely acclaimed book by an award-winning author, this tells the story of Michael who moves house with his parents and sick sister. In the crumbling garage he finds a creature. Is it human or something else? It's a tender story of a family facing a life-threatening illness, and laced throughout with love and faith. It is underpinned by the theme of resilience and the need to find sustaining resources in the face of uncertainty.

The Tale of Two Dolphins: When My Sister Died Suddenly by Sarah Fitzgerald, illustrated by Kate Galle, Brambles Press, 2000

Sarah, the young author, wrote this book after her sister died in a tragic M40 school minibus crash. She tells the simple story of two sister dolphins, one called Claire and one called Sarah. Claire gets caught in fishing nets that kill her. After this, another dolphin called Laura helps Sarah by playing with her, having fun with her but also encouraging Sarah to talk about her sad feelings. The book ends by affirming that Claire, the dolphin, would never be forgotten. An excellent book written from the heart by a young person who shares her journey through grief with others. It is particularly helpful for children who have experienced the death of a sibling.

Millions by Frank Cottrell Boyce, illustrated by Steven Lenton, Macmillan Children's Books, 2004

This Carnegie Medal-winning book tells the story of the Cunningham brothers who find a sack full of money, days before the Euro is introduced. They must spend the money soon and before the robbers find them. Their hilarious adventure leads them to discover what brings happiness and to realise that money can never bring back their mother who has died. It is a life-affirming book that deals with grief, family dynamics and continuing bonds.

Pizza on Saturday by R. Anderson, Hodder, 2004

Charlotte's world changes suddenly when her father suffers a devastating stroke. She learns that nothing stays the same after this, including herself, as she meets new people who have their own problems, including a girl who has travelled from across the world in terrifying circumstances. Bereavement is central to this short, easy-to-read novel.

Tiger Eyes by Judy Blume, Delacorte Press, 1981

Fifteen-year-old Davey has to cope with the traumatic impact of the killing of her father during a shop raid. Her losses are cumulative as her mother moves the family across America, and she loses her place, her friends and her school. The book deals with feelings of fear, rage and grief, and shows how Davey manages to cope with her radically changed life.

Ways to Live Forever by Sally Nicholls, Marion Lloyd Books, 2008

Sam is dying of acute lymphoblastic leukaemia, and the book is about what he wants to do before he dies. He makes a list that includes going up a down escalator and seeing the earth from space, and with his friend he has a series of adventures. It is a very readable book that deals sensitively and humorously with coming to terms with treatment, refusing it eventually, and death and its impact on the family. An award-winning book that is an engaging read.

BOOKS FOR 13- TO 16-YEAR-OLDS

A Summer to Die by Lois Lowry, illustrated by Jenni Oliver, Houghton Mifflin, 1977

Sisters Meg and Molly are not pleased when the family moves to the country and the girls have to share a bedroom. Molly, the elder sister, is diagnosed with acute myeloid leukaemia and the story charts the siblings' relationship as Molly moves towards death. It also shows how Meg accepts that bad things can happen to good people and recovers love despite having had sibling rivalry issues. In writing the novel, Lowry drew on her own experience of the death of her sister at a young age.

I Never Told Her I Loved Her by Sandra Chick, Livewire Books for Teenagers, 1997

When Frankie's mother dies, she struggles because all she can remember are the arguments they had and the quarrels of her parents. Gradually, Frankie and her father talk about what happened and their feelings, and find a way to move on. It shows how feelings of guilt and regret can impact on bereaved young people.

On Eagles' Wings by Sue Mayfield, Lion Children's Books, 2004

Tony's mother is dying. There is nothing he can do about it and he can't always keep his feelings under control. Part of him just wishes he could fly away like an eagle, soar into the sky and be free. Little by little, he begins to understand that death can bring freedom. This is a book about growing up, family relationships and anticipatory grief.

The Charlie Barber Treatment by Carole Lloyd, Walker Books Ltd, 1990

Simon comes home from school to find out that his mother has died suddenly of a brain haemorrhage. With his GCSE coursework piling up and now having to help around the house, he finds his teenage life radically changed. He doesn't go out with his friends much and times are tough. One day he meets Charlie when she is visiting her grandma. She believes fate has brought them together and Simon starts to enjoy life again and to re-build relationships with family and friends. This is a sensitive book that reflects the thoughts and emotions of a teenage boy.

The Lost Boys' Appreciation Society by Alan Gibbons, Orion Children's Books, 2007

Teenage life for Gary and John is difficult enough, but when their mother dies in a car crash, things get worse. John struggles to keep the peace as his brother Gary goes off the rails, saying his new mates are his family now. GCSE exams are looming, and with dad going out on dates, things get overwhelming for John. This vivid book conveys some of the feelings and problems in relationships following bereavement, and how different people react to major life events.

Up on Cloud Nine by Anne Fine, Corgi Children's Books, 2006

Stolly falls out of a top floor window and ends up unconscious in hospital with lots of injuries. No one knows if Stolly has had an accident or had made a suicide attempt. The book is told from the perspective of Ian, his best friend, as he sits by his friend's bedside. He recalls all the good times they had together as well as recognising the slightly different way Stolly sees the world. Ian also captures the emotions of his own adoptive parents as well as Stolly's family and the hospital staff in an amusing way, showing how Stolly has had an inspirational effect on the lives he touches.

Minty by Christina Banach, Three Hares Publishing, 2014

Minty and Jess are 14-year-old twins who are inseparable; however, the sea claims Minty as she tries to rescue her dog. It is a moving ghost story told from the point of view of the ghost, Minty, who is trapped in limbo and has to watch the devastation her death causes for those who are left behind. It shows how each person copes with bereavement, and is balanced between sadness and lightness as well as being humorous. There is also a strong sense of spirituality in the book. It aims to leave the reader with a sense of hope.

How to Look for a Lost Dog by Ann M. Martin, Usborne Publishing, 2014

This is the story of Rose Howard, a nearly 14-year-old, who loses her dog Rain and discovers both loss and enduring love. Rose has autism and loves homonyms. It is a rare find to discover a book that has a character with specific needs that also deals with bereavement and loss in such a creative and touching way. There is a twist in the tale that I won't give away, but it deals sensitively with the complexities of loss in its myriad of forms. Beautifully written, it moved me to tears.

The Fault in Our Stars by John Green, Penguin, 2012

Sixteen-year-old Hazel has a terminal illness. At the Cancer Kids Support Group she meets Augustus Waters, who is in remission from cancer. It is a quintessential teenage love story that tackles real issues around illness, loss and death. It has had huge acclaim and has been made into a film.

The Lie Tree by Frances Hardinge, Macmillan, 2015

Faith's father is found dead in mysterious circumstances and she has to make sense of the journals he leaves behind. This dark tale for older readers won the Costa book of the year in 2015, and includes a great deal of information on Victorian funeral rites and the social attitude to suicide at that time, as well as a myriad of emotions following a sudden death.

Straight Talk about Death for Teenagers: How to Cope with Losing Someone You Love by Earl A. Grollman, Beacon Press, 1993

This well-written book is for teenagers to read themselves. It deals with emotions and reactions to death, rituals that can help, as well as managing special days and anniversaries. It explains what to expect when you lose someone you love.

Grief is the Thing with Feathers by Max Porter, Faber & Faber, 2015

The author was six years old when his father died at the age of 37. This novel describes the events following the sudden death of the main character's wife as he and his two young sons grapple with the aftermath of her death. Central to the story is Crow, who comes to visit the home of the Ted Hughes scholar, and is a mixture of a trickster and protector and who won't leave until they don't need him anymore. Somehow Crow leads them through their accommodation of their loss. The language spits and reels as a response to the devastating impact the death has on them. Porter tells the story through the voices of the father, the two boys and the crow. 'Moving on, as a concept, is for stupid people, because any sensible person knows grief is a long term project. I refuse to rush. The pain that is thrust upon us let no man slow or speed or fix' (p.99).

ONLINE FORUMS FOR CONNECTION AND CONVERSATIONS

There are a huge variety of resources available on the internet about death and bereavement that offer support and information. There are specialised sites for memorials that continue the bonds between the living and those who have died. I have included a selection here, but as always, check the sites yourself first (Sanders 2011).

Births, Marriages and Deaths

www.bmdsonline.co.uk

> This is a forum where people may leave testimonies about their deceased loved ones and share their stories. It provides the opportunity to light a candle, post a message or a treasured image, animate a message, share a slide show, and invite others to share videos.

Child Bereavement UK

www.childbereavementuk.org

> Child Bereavement UK supports families when a baby or a child of any age dies or is dying. It also helps children who are facing bereavement. It offers training in bereavement support to those working on the front line with children and families.

Childhood Bereavement Network

www.childhoodbereavementnetwork.org.uk

This provides a directory of resources around the country that offer bereavement services to families and young people. It also offers information and training and has publications that can be purchased.

The Compassionate Friends

www.tcf.org.uk

This is an organisation of bereaved parents, siblings and grandparents that offers support and compassion to those affected by the death of a child of any age from any cause. It has a helpline, an online members' forum as well as local groups throughout the UK.

Macmillan

www.macmillan.org.uk

Macmillan Cancer Support helps anyone who is affected by cancer, either their own illness or a family member.

Child Death Helpline

www.childdeathhelpline.org

This is a freephone service that is available every day of the year where trained volunteers, who are all bereaved parents, offer support. It is for anyone affected by the death of a child of any age, including stillbirth, in whatever circumstances.

Riprap

www.riprap.org.uk

Riprap offers support to 12- to 16-year-olds whose parent has cancer. There are forums, personal accounts by young people and their feelings and reactions to the illness and treatment of their loved ones. There are videos of young people talking, and young people are offered the opportunity to get personal support from others who share their experience.

Hope Again

http://hopeagain.org.uk

> The oldest interactive site for children and young people, rd4u, was developed in 2001 by Cruse Bereavement Care. Now called Hope Again, it is for children and young people to communicate with each other, to share their stories, fears and feelings; this helps bereaved children to feel less isolated and more supported by others. There is a general message board, a gallery where they can upload images, post memorials and watch videos where they talk about their experiences. As with other websites, there is information about grieving and helpful material that can be printed off. It also has a direct link to trained volunteers who can be contacted by email or through the telephone helpline.

Winston's Wish

www.winstonswish.org.uk

> Winston's Wish, the leading UK bereavement charity for children and young people, has an interactive site that offers resources to support bereaved children, family and professionals. It includes a graffiti wall where 'spray cans' can be used to draw messages, and a 'Skyscape of memories', where the young person can attach messages or memories to stars that shine in the night sky. This helps the child build continuing bonds with the person who has died. There are also blogs, podcasts and an interactive section.

Seeds of Hope

http://seedsofhopechildrensgarden.co.uk

> The Seeds of Hope site is a garden where children can explore the four seasons: Spring, the Garden of Hope; Summer, the Garden of Light; Autumn, the Garden of Change; and Winter, the Garden of Thought. Caroline Jay, who also founded the charity, created this garden in the grounds of Guildford Cathedral, and offers tours and activities for children and school trips to explore the cycle of life, loss and regeneration. Children can plant memories on the website. There is an activity book that offers a great number of resources to help children experiencing loss.

Brake

www.brake.org.uk

Brake is the road safety charity that offers care and support to those who have been bereaved or affected by a road traffic collision. It has two useful booklets for children who have been suddenly bereaved. It also has information about road safety, organises campaigns and has a memorial site where people can post tributes about the person who has died following a road traffic collision.

SAMM, Support After Murder & Manslaughter

www.samm.org.uk

This offers emotional support to those bereaved by murder or manslaughter. It also provides advice and training to many agencies on issues relevant to the traumatically bereaved.

Survivors of Bereavement by Suicide

www.uk-sobs.org.uk

This is a self-help organisation that offers support to those affected by death by suicide. It aims to meet the needs of anyone affected, and to break down the isolation many people experience following a death in this manner.

KidsAid

http://kidsaid.com

The American-based website is '2 kids, 4 kids, By Kids'. It offers a gallery of stories, a section on animal loss, a question and answer section and space for stories and artwork.

What's Your Grief?

https://whatsyourgrief.com

This offers resources and has sections on 'Creative coping', 'Holidays' and 'Special days', a blog as well as sections on books, music and movies.

Grieving Students

www.grievingstudents.org

> This American site has videos including commentaries from school professionals, as well as bereaved parents and family members, and resources that can be downloaded.

Grief Works

https://griefworks.co.uk

> This site was set up by the grief psychotherapist and author Julia Samuel, and has links to support sites, information and forums where people can exchange information.

APPS FOR YOUNG PEOPLE

www.childbereavementuk.org/our-app

> This app has information about bereavement, grief, feelings and how others can help.

www.nelsonsjourney.org.uk

> Smiles and Tears app, for sharing memories and remembering a special person.

References

Adams, K. (2004) 'Divine dreams through a child's eyes.' *Dreams: International Association for the Study of Dreams*, Winter, 4–7.

Adams, K. (2016) 'Divine Dreams: Religious and Spiritual Themes.' In C.R. Johnson and J.M. Campbell (eds) *Sleep Monsters and Superheroes: Empowering Children through Creative Dreamplay* (pp.211–226). Santa Barbara, CA: Praeger.

Adams, K. and Hyde, B. (2008) 'Children's grief dreams and the theory of spiritual intelligence.' *Dreams: International Association for the Study of Dreams 18*, 1, 58–67.

Adams, K., Hyde, B. and Wooley, R. (2008) *The Spiritual Dimension of Childhood*. London: Jessica Kingsley Publishers.

Albom, M. (2002) *Tuesdays with Morrie: An Old Man, a Young Man and Life's Greatest Lesson*. New York: Random House.

All Party Parliamentary Group on Arts, Health and Wellbeing Inquiry (2017) *Creative Health: The Arts for Health and Wellbeing. The Short Report*. July, pp.1–14.

Almond, D. (2000) *Counting Stars*. London: Hodder.

Anderson, R. (1974) 'Notes of a Survivor.' In S.B. Troop and W.A. Green (eds) *The Patient, Death, and the Family* (pp.73–82). New York: Scribner.

Arens, G. (2006) 'Support for siblings: Group work with the siblings of life-limited and terminally ill children has a major impact on their emotional resilience.' *Therapy Today*, June, 42–46.

Ariès, P. (1974) *Western Attitudes towards Death: From the Middle Ages to the Present*. Baltimore, MD and London: Johns Hopkins University Press.

Atwater, P.M.H. (1999) *Children of the New Millennium: Children's Near Death Experiences and the Evolution of Humankind*. New York: Three Rivers Press.

Balk, D.E. (1999) 'Bereavement and spiritual change.' *Death Studies*, September, 23, 6, 485–493.

Bank, S.P. and Kahn, M.D. (1982) *The Sibling Bond*. New York: Basic Books.

Barnes, J., Kroll, L., Burke, O., Lee, J., Jones, A. and Stein, A. (2000) 'Qualitative interview study of communication between parents and children about maternal breast cancer.' *British Medical Journal 321*, 479–482.

Barrett, D. (1992) 'Through a glass darkly: Images of the dead in dreams.' *Omega – Journal of Death and Dying 24*, 2, 97–108.

Bassett, D.J. (2015) 'Who wants to live forever? Living, dying and grieving in our digital society.' *Social Sciences 4*, 4, 1121–1139.

Batten, M. and Oltjenbruns, K.A. (1999) 'Adolescent sibling bereavement as a catalyst for spiritual development: A model for understanding.' *Death Studies*, September, 23, 6, 529–546.

Baum, L.F. (1982) *The Wizard of Oz*. London: Puffin Classics.

Becker, S.H. and Knudson, R.M. (2003) 'Visions of the dead: Imagination and mourning.' *Death Studies 27*, 691–716.

Bell, J., Bailey, L. and Kennedy, D. (2015) '"We do it to keep him alive": Bereaved individuals' experience of online suicide memorials and continuing bonds.' *Mortality 20*, 5, 375–389.

Bellous, J.E. (ed.) (2010) *Children, Spirituality, Loss and Recovery*. Abingdon: Routledge.

Berry, E. (2017). *Stranger, Baby*. London: Faber & Faber.

Blackman, N. (2003) *Loss and Learning Disability*. London: Worth.

Bosacki, S. (2001) '"Theory of Mind or Theory of the Soul?" The Role of Spirituality in Children's Understanding of Minds and Emotions.' In J. Erricker, C. Ota and C. Erricker (eds) *Spiritual Education: Cultural, Religious and Social Differences, New Perspectives for the 21st Century* (pp.156–169). Brighton: Sussex Academic.

Brake (2011) Supporting Suddenly Bereaved Children and Young People Seminar, July. London.

Brams-Prudeaux, J. (2005) 'The Gift of Loss.' Encino, CA: Psychotherapy & Meditation Center.

Brennan, F. and Dash, M. (2009) 'The year of magical thinking: Joan Didion and the dialectic of grief.' *Bereavement Care 28*, 2, 31–36.

Brooks, R. and Goldstein, S. (2001) *Raising a Resilient Child: Fostering Strength, Hope and Optimism in Our Children*. New York: Contemporary Books.

Brown, R. (2013) 'An artistic cancer journey.' ehospice, 20 August. Accessed on 8/12/2017 at www.ehospice.com/ArticleView/tabid/10697/ArticleId/6236/View.aspx

Buchan, C. (2007) 'Obituary: Michele Angelo Petrone.' *The Lancet 369*, 30 June. Accessed on 12/10/2017 at www.thelancet.com/pdfs/journals/lancet/PIIS0140673607609994.pdf

Bulkeley, K. (2000) *Transforming Dreams: Learning Spiritual Lessons from the Dreams You Never Forget*. New York: Wiley.

Bulkeley, K. and Bulkeley, P. (2005) *Dreaming Beyond Death: A Guide to Pre-death Dreams and Visions*. Boston, MA: Beacon Press.

Bulkeley, K. and Bulkley, P. (2016) 'Nightmares as a Gift: The Surprising Value of Frightening Dreams in Childhood.' In C.R. Johnson and J.M. Campbell (eds) *Sleep Monsters and Superheroes: Empowering Children through Creative Dreamplay* (pp.21–33). Santa Barbara, CA: Praeger.

Bull, A., Reverend (2007) *The Spiritual Needs of Hospitalised School-aged Children with Complex Healthcare Needs*. London: Jessica Kingsley Publishers.

Bycock, I. (1997) *Dying Well: The Prospect for Growth at the End of Life*. New York: Riverhead Books.

Bycock, I. (2013) 'Saying the Four Things that Matter Most for Living and Dying Well.' Presentation at National Palliative Care Week, Melbourne, VIC.

Bycock, I. (2014) *The Four Things that Matter Most: A Book about Living*. New York: Simon & Schuster.

Bylund-Grenko, T., Kreicbergs, U., Uggla, C., Valdimarsdóttir, U.A., Nyberg, T., Steineck, G. and Fürst, C.J. (2014) 'Teenagers want to be told when a parent's death is near. A nationwide study of cancer-bereaved youths' opinions and experiences.' *Acta Oncologica 54*, 6, 944–950.

Campanella, L. (2017) *When All That's Left of Me Is Love: A Daughter's Story of Letting Go.* Campanella Books.

Campbell, J. (1993) *The Hero with a Thousand Faces.* London: Fontana Press.

Carey, J. (2005) *What Good Are the Arts?* London: Faber & Faber.

Carey, T. (2016) 'Mum's bucket list: "Have a great time after I've gone".' *The Guardian*, 19 November. Accessed on 12/10/2017 at www.theguardian. com/lifeandstyle/2016/nov/19/mums-list-film-kate-greene-bucket-list-family

CBN (Child Bereavement Network) (2016) 'Key estimated statistics on childhood bereavement.' London: CBN. Accessed on 28/4/2017 at www. childhoodbereavementnetwork.org.uk/research/key-statistics.aspx

CBN (2017) 'One thing I'd like you to know...' London: CBN. Accessed on 26/7/2017 at www.childhoodbereavementnetwork.org.uk/help-around-a-death/young-peoples-stories/story-6.aspx

CBN (no date) 'Grief Matters for Children.' London: CBN. Accessed on 10/10/2017 at www.childhoodbereavementnetwork.org.uk/media/57656/ Grief-Matters-for-Children-2017.pdf

CBUK (Child Bereavement UK) (2017) 'Death of a sibling: Daniel Tse.' Saunderton: CBUK. Accessed on 15/8/2017 at https://childbereavementuk. org/for-families/family-stories/death-of-a-sibling

CBUK (2017a) 'Death of a parent: Mithra Nandoo.' Saunderton: CBUK. Accessed on 15/8/2017 at https://childbereavementuk.org/for-families/ family-stories/death-of-a-parent

CBUK (2017b) 'Death of a sibling: Tabitha Symonds.' Saunderton: CBUK. Accessed on 15/8/2017 at https://childbereavementuk.org/for-families/ family-stories/death-of-a-sibling

CBUK (2017c) 'Managing Christmas.' Saunderton: CBUK. Accessed on 10/10/2017 at https://childbereavementuk.org/for-families/specific-areas-support/managing-special-occasions/managing-christmas

Chan, C., Chow, A., Ho, S., Tsui, Y., Koo, B. and Koo, E. (2005) 'The experience of Chinese bereaved persons: A preliminary study of meaning making and continuing bonds.' *Death Studies 10*, 29, 923–947.

Chochinov, H.M. (2003) 'Thinking outside the box: Depression, hope and meaning at the end of life.' *Journal of Palliative Medicine 6*, 6, December, 973–977.

Chowns, G. (2013) '"Until it ends, you never know..." Attending to the voice of adolescents who are facing the likely death of a parent.' *Bereavement Care 31*, 1, 23–30.

Christ, G.H. (2000) *Healing Children's Grief: Surviving a Parent's Death from Cancer.* Oxford: Oxford University Press.

Co-Operative Funeral Care (2015) *Funeral Trends 2015: The Ways We Say Goodbye.* Media Report. Accessed on 10/10/2017 at https://assets.contentful. com/5ywmq66472jr/4agQrKl0bueAal8o2MlQ04/9b5f9a228e04bc5ecc 2f8ecb74a0af91/Ways_We_Say_Goodbye_FINAL.pdf

Corr, C.A. and Balk, D.E. (eds) (2010) *Children's Encounters with Death, Bereavement and Coping.* New York: Springer.

Cranwell, B. (2007) 'Adult decisions affecting bereaved children: Researching the children's perspective.' *Bereavement Care 26*, 2, 30–33.

Cranwell, B. (2010) *Where's My Mum Now? Children's Perspectives on Helps and Hindrances to Their Grief*. Milton Keynes: AuthorHouse.

Crossley, D. (2000) *Muddles, Puddles and Sunshine*. Gloucester: Winston's Wish Publications.

Darling, D. (1995) *Soul Search: A Scientist Explores the Afterlife*. New York: Villard Books.

Davies, B. (2014) 'When life sends you lemons.' *Mslexia*, June/July/August, 15–16.

Davies, C. (2017) 'Prince Harry: I regret not talking about my mother's death sooner.' *The Guardian*, 25 July.

Devita-Raeburn, E. (2004) *The Empty Room: Surviving the Loss of a Brother or Sister at Any Age*. New York: Scribner.

Di Ciacco, J.A. (2008) *The Colors of Grief: Understanding a Child's Journey through Loss from Birth to Adulthood*. London: Jessica Kingsley Publishers.

Didion, J. (2005) *The Year of Magical Thinking*. London: Fourth Estate.

Donnelly, J. (ed.) (1994) *Language, Metaphyisics and Death* (2nd edn). New York: Fordham University Press.

Dougy Center, The (2017) 'Pathways program for families facing an advanced serious illness.' Portland, OR: The Dougy Center. Accessed on 10/10/2017 at www.dougy.org/news-events/news/pathways-program-for-families-facing-an-advanced-serious-illness/1577

Draper, A. (2008) *Good Grief: What Will We Tell the Kids?* West Hertfordshire Primary Care Trust. Accessed on 20/8/2017 at www.thegrid.org.uk/learning/hwb/ewb/resources/documents/good_grief.pdf

Duerden, N. (2011) 'David Servan-Schrieber: "He was not afraid of death".' *The Guardian*, Obituary, 3 December, Family Section, p.1.

Dyregrov, A. (2008) *Grief in Children: A Handbook for Adults*. London: Jessica Kingsley Publishers.

Emmons, R.A. and McCullough, M.E. (2003) 'Counting blessings versus burdens: An experiential investigation of gratitude and subjective well-being in daily life.' *Journal of Personality and Social Psychology 84*, 2, 377–389.

Fairfield, P. (1915) *Death: A Philosophical Inquiry*. London: Routledge.

Fenwick, P. and Fenwick, E. (1995) *The Truth in the Light: An Investigation of Over 300 Near-Death Experiences*. Guildford: White Crow Books.

Ferrell, B.R. and Coyle, N. (2001) *Oxford Textbook of Palliative Nursing*. Oxford: Oxford University Press.

Ferris, L.R. (2016) 'Bereavement round up: Digital legacies.' *Bereavement Care 35*, 1, 41–42.

Fitzgerald, S. (1999) *The Tale of Two Dolphins: When My Sister Died Suddenly* (K. Galle, illustrator). Worcs.: Bramble's Press.

Forward, D.R. and Garlie, N. (2003) 'Search for new meaning: Adolescent bereavement after the sudden death of a sibling.' *Canadian Journal of School Psychology 18*, 1–2, 23–52.

Foster, T.L., Contreras, R., Gordon, J.E., Roth, M. and Gilmer, M.J. (2012) 'Continuing bonds reported by bereaved individuals in Ecuador.' *Bereavement Care 31*, 3, 120–128.

Fox, J. (1995) *When Someone Deeply Listens to You*. New York: Tarcher.

Fuller, A. (2009) 'The unexpected gifts of loss.' *Bereavement Care 28*, 3, 2–4.

Gaines, A.G. and Polsky, M.E. (2017) *I Have a Question about Death: A Book for Children with Autism Spectrum Disorder or Other Special Needs*. London: Jessica Kingsley Publishers.

Garfield, P. (1997) *The Dream Messenger: How Dreams of the Departed Bring Healing Gifts*. New York: Simon & Schuster.

Gladwell, M. (2013) *David and Goliath: Underdogs, Misfits and the Art of Battling Giants*. New York: Back Bay Books.

Glover, E., Phillips, V., Rice, G. and Williamson, C. (2016) 'Shadow into light: A Bristol-based arts project for bereavement.' *Bereavement Care 35*, 1, 7–12.

Golightly, A. (2016) 'Widower of the parish.' *The Guardian*, 17 December, p.7.

Gopnik, A., Meltzoff, A.N. and Kuhl, P.K. (1999) *The Scientist in the Crib: Minds, Brains and How Children Learn*. New York: William Morrow.

Gordon, J. (1995) 'Grieving Together: Helping Family Members Share Their Grief.' In S.C. Smith and Sister M. Pennells (eds) *Interventions with Bereaved Children* (pp.121–138). London: Jessica Kingsley Publishers.

Graves, D. (2009) *Talking with Bereaved People: An Approach for Structured and Sensitive Communication*. London: Jessica Kingsley Publishers.

Gray, S. (2011) 'The alchemy of words.' *Bereavement Care 30*, 1, 2–4.

Greene, St J. (2012) *Mum's List: A Mother's Life Lessons to the Husband and Sons She Left Behind*. London: Penguin Books.

Grimmitt, M., Grove, J. and Spencer, L. (1991) *A Gift to the Child: Religious Experience in the Primary School*. London: Simon & Schuster.

Grosz, S. (2013) *The Examined Life: How We Lose and Find Ourselves*. London: Chatto & Windus.

Hall, C.W. (2011) 'After the firestorm: Supporting bereaved people following the 2009 Victorian bushfires.' *Bereavement Care 30*, 2, July, 5–9.

Hardinge, F. (2015) *The Lie Tree*. Basingstoke: Macmillan.

Harrison, R. (2002) *Ordinary Days and Shattered Lives: Sudden Death and the Impact on Children and Families*. West Wycombe: Child Bereavement Trust.

Hartman, E. and Basile, R. (2003) 'Dream imagery becomes more intense after 9/11/01.' *Dreaming: The Journal of the Association for the Study of Dreams 13*, 2, June, 61–66.

Hay, D. and Nye, R. (2006) *The Spirit of the Child* (revised edn). London: Jessica Kingsley Publishers.

Heaney, S. (1998) 'Mid-Term Break.' *Opened Ground: Selected Poems 1966–1996*. New York: Farrar, Straus & Giroux.

Hedges, D. (2015) *Poetry, Therapy and Emotional Life*. Oxford: Radcliffe.

Hedtke, L. (2000) 'Dancing with death.' *Gecko: A Journal of Deconstruction and Narrative Ideas in Therapeutic Practice 2*, 5–16.

Hirooka, K., Fukahori, H., Akita, Y. and Ozawa, M. (2017) 'Posttraumatic growth among Japanese parentally bereaved adolescents: A web-based survey.' *The American Journal of Hospice & Palliative Care 34*, 5, June, 442–448.

Horwitz, T. (2002) *Blue Latitudes: Boldly Going Where Captain Cook Has Gone Before*. New York: Picador.

Hoyle, E. (2012) 'Life without Geoff.' *Bereavement Care 31*, 3, 96–97.

Huffington, A. (2014) *Thrive: The Third Metric to Redefining Success and Creating a Happier Life*. London: W.H. Allen.

Hugo, V. (1862) *Les Misérables*, Chapter IV, Madeleine in Mourning. New York: Carleton Publishers.

Ishida, M., Onishi, H., Wada, M., Wada, T., Uchitomi, Y. and Nomura, S. (2010) 'Bereavement dream? Successful antidepressant treatment for bereavement-related distressing dreams in patients with major depression.' *Palliative Supportive Care* 8, 1, 95–98.

ITV (2017) 'Diana, Our Mother: Her Life and Legacy.' Interview with Prince Harry, 24 July.

Jacobs, W.J. (1991) *Mother Theresa: Helping the Poor*. Minneapolis, MN: Lerner Publications.

Jeffers, O. (2016) 'Summer books.' *The Guardian*, 9 July, p.4.

Joseph, S. (2013) *What Doesn't Kill Us: A Guide to Overcoming Adversity and Moving Forward.* London: Piatkus.

Kabat-Zinn, J. (1990) *Full Catastrophe Living: How to Cope with Stress, Pain and Illness Using Mindfulness Meditation*. London: Piatkus.

Kay, J. (2017) *Ten Poems of Kindness.* Nottingham: Candlestick Press.

Kellaway, J. (2017) 'Grief works: Stories of life, death and surviving – Review.' *The Guardian*, 12 March. Accessed on 12/10/2017 at www.theguardian.com/books/2017/mar/12/grief-works-stories-life-death-and-surviving-review-julia-samuel

Klass, D. (1999) *The Spiritual Lives of Bereaved Parents*. Philadelphia, PA: Brunner/Mazel.

Klass, D., Silverman, P.R. and Nickman, S.L. (eds) (1996) *Continuing Bonds: New Understandings of Grief*. London: Taylor & Francis.

Kleinman, A. (2016) 'Caring for memories.' *Bereavement Care 35*, 2, Summer.

Koehler, K. (2016) 'Supporting children and young people with Autistic Spectrum Disorder.' *Bereavement Care 35*, 3, Winter, 94–101.

Krause, N. and Bastida, E. (2010) 'Exploring the interface between religion and contact with the dead among older Mexican Americans.' *Review of Religious Research 51*, 1, 5–20.

Kübler-Ross, E. (1975) *Death: The Final Stage of Growth*. New York: Simon & Schuster.

Kübler-Ross, E. (1985) *On Children and Death*. New York: Collier Books, Macmillan.

Laity, P. (2017) 'Paul Auster: "I'm going to speak out as often as I can, otherwise I can't live with myself".' *The Guardian*, 20 January. Accessed on 1/11/2017 at www.theguardian.com/books/2017/jan/20/paul-auster-4321-interview

Lemon, M. (2017) 'My dad's murder didn't break me.' *The Guardian*, Family, 3 June, pp.4–5.

Lewis, C.S. (1961) *A Grief Observed*. London: Faber & Faber.

Lipskey, D. (2013) *How People with Autism Grieve, and How to Help: An Insider Handbook*. London: Jessica Kingsley Publishers.

LoConto, D.G. (1998) 'Death and dreams: A sociological approach to grieving and identity.' *Omega 37*, 171–185.

Lowry, L. (2002) 'The remembered gate and the unopened door.' *Horn Book Magazine 78*, 2, 159–177.

MacConville, U. (2010) 'Roadside memorials: Making grief visible.' *Bereavement Care 29*, 3, 34–36.

Macpherson, C. (2017) 'Difficulties for a practitioner preparing a family for the death of a parent: A narrative enquiry.' *Mortality*, 20 June, 1–14. Accessed on 10/10/2017 at http://dx.doi.org/10.1080/13576275.2017.1339677

Maddrell, A. (2012) 'Online memorials: The virtual as the new vernacular.' *Bereavement Care 31*, 2, 46–54.

Mallon, B. (1989) *Children Dreaming: Pictures in my Pillow*. London: Penguin.

Mallon, B. (1998) *Helping Children to Manage Loss: Positive Strategies for Renewal and Growth*. London: Jessica Kingsley Publishers.

Mallon, B. (2000) *Dreams, Counselling and Healing*. Dublin: Gill & MacMillan Ltd.

Mallon, B. (2002) *Dream Time with Children*. London: Jessica Kingsley Publishers.

Mallon, B. (2009) *Death, Dying and Grief: Working with Adult Bereavement*. London: Sage.

Mallon, B. (2011) *Working with Bereaved Children and Young People*. London: Sage.

Mantel, H. (2017) 'The princess myth: Hilary Mantel on Diana.' *The Guardian*, Review, 26 August, pp.2–4.

Marshall, E. (2003) *Kids Talk about Heaven*. London: Kyle Cathie Ltd.

Martin, A.M. (2016) *How to Look for a Lost Dog*. London: Usborne Publishing.

Maslow, A. (1943) 'A theory of human motivation.' *Psychological Review 50*, 4, 370–396.

McArdle, S. and Byrt, R. (2001) 'Fiction, poetry and mental health: Expressive and therapeutic uses of literature.' *Journal of Psychiatric and Mental Health Nursing 8*, 6, 517–524.

Mistiaen, V. (1999) 'A young girl's allegory helps others surface from grief.' *The Chicago Tribune*, 24 October.

Mitchell, J. (2017) 'What will survive of us is love – An interview with Cathy Phelan.' *Bereavement Care 36*, 1, Spring, 2–7.

Moore, K. (2009) 'One woman and her dog.' *Bereavement Care 28*, 3, 25–28.

Monroe, B. and Oliviere, D. (eds) (2007) *Resilience in Palliative Care: Achievement in Adversity*. Oxford: Oxford University Press.

Moorjani, A. (2012) *Dying to Be Me: My Journey from Cancer, to Near Death, to True Healing*. London: Hay House.

Morpurgo, M. (2006) 'Aunt Bessie's stocking forest.' *The Guardian*, 14 January. Accessed on 11/10/2017 at www.theguardian.com/lifeandstyle/2006/jan/14/familyandrelationships.family1

Moss, J. (2010) 'Sunflowers on the road to NASA.' Spotlight on Practice. *Bereavement Care 29*, 2, 24, 1–11.

Moss, J. (2012) *Writing in Bereavement*. London: Jessica Kingsley Publishers.

Neimeyer, R.A. (ed.) (2012) *Techniques of Grief Therapy: Creative Practices for Counselling the Bereaved*. London: Routledge.

Neimeyer, R.A., Baldwin, S.A. and Gillies, J. (2006) 'Continuing bonds and reconstructing meaning: Mitigating complications in bereavement.' *Death Studies 8*, 30, 715–738.

Ness, P. (2011) *A Monster Calls*. London: Walker Books.

ONS (Office for National Statistics) (2016) 'Deaths.' Accessed on 1/11/2017 at www.ons.gov.uk/peoplepopulationandcommunity/births deathsandmarriages/deaths

Packman, W., Horsley, H., Davies, B. and Kramer, R. (2006) 'Sibling bereavement and continuing bonds.' *Death Studies 3*, 817–881.

Parkes, C.M. (1988) 'A new paradigm for grief.' *Bereavement Care 17*, 2, Summer, 28.

Pascoe, J. (2003) *Our Father Who Art in a Tree*. London: Random House.

Pennebaker, J.W. (1997) 'Writing about emotional experiences as a therapeutic process.' *Psychological Science 8*, 3, 162–166.

Pennebaker, J.W. (2004) *Writing to Heal: A Guided Journal for Recovering from Trauma and Emotional Upheaval*. Oakland, CA: New Harbinger Publications.

Petrone, M.A. (1999) *Touching the Rainbow: Pictures and Words by People Affected by Cancer*. Bexhill-on-Sea: East Sussex Health Promotion Department.

Petrone, M.A. (2000) Michele Angelo Petrone Art workshop. Manchester: Owen's Park, Annual Cancer Conference, June.

Petrone, M.A. (2003) *The Emotional Cancer Journey*. Brighton: MAP Foundation.

Pollack, W.S. (2006) 'Creating Genuine Resilience in Boys and Young Males.' In S. Goldstein and R. Brooks (eds) *Handbook of Resilience in Children* (pp.65–78). New York: Springer Science and Business Media.

Porter, M. (2015) *Grief is the Thing with Feathers*. London: Faber & Faber.

Proust, M. (2005) *In Search of Lost Time. Volume 1: Swan's Way*. Translated by C.K.S. Moncrieff and T. Kilmartin. London: Chatto and Windus.

Ribbens McCarthy, J. (2006) *Young People's Experiences of Loss and Bereavement: Towards an Interdisciplinary Approach*. London: Open University Press.

Ribbens McCarthy, J. and Jessop, J. (2005) *Young People, Bereavement and Loss: Disruptive Transitions?* London: National Children's Bureau.

Riches, G. and Dawson, P. (2000) *An Intimate Loneliness: Supporting Bereaved Parents and Siblings*. Milton Keynes: Open University Press.

Roberts, P. (2012) '"2 people like this": Mourning according to format.' *Bereavement Care 31*, 2, 55–61.

Rosen, H. (1988) *Unspoken Grief*. Toronto, ON: Lexington Books.

Round, S. (2013) Interview: 'Stephen Grosz: Telling tales from the consulting room.' *The Jewish Chronicle*, 14 March. Accessed on 1/11/2017 at www.thejc.com/lifestyle/interviews/stephen-grosz-telling-tales-from-the-consulting-room-1.42936

Rowling, J.K. (1997) *Harry Potter and the Philosopher's Stone*. London: Bloomsbury Publishing.

Sacks, O. (1985) *The Man Who Mistook His Wife for a Hat*. London: Gerald Duckworth.

Sacks, O. (2010) *The Mind's Eye*. London: Macmillan.

Sanders, J. (2011) 'Bereavement websites for children and young people.' *Bereavement Care 30*, 2, July, 33–35.

Saner, E. (2017) 'Paul Chowdhry.' *The Guardian*, 5 August, p.30.

Saner, E. (2017a) 'You've been given a brain – use it.' *The Guardian*, G2, 28 August, pp.6–8.

Samuel, J. (2017) *Grief Works: Stories of Life, Death and Surviving*. London: Penguin.

Sartori, P. (2014) *The Wisdom of Near-Death Experiences: How Understanding NDEs Can Help Us Live More Fully*. Oxford: Watkins Publishers Ltd.

Schonfeld, D.J. and Demaria, T. (2016) 'Supporting the grieving child and family.' *Pediatrics 138*, 3, September, e20162147.

Scott, D. (2016) 'Relative values: Felix and Hugo White, of The Maccabees.' *The Sunday Times*, 3 January. Accessed on 12/10/2017 at www.thetimes. co.uk/article/relative-values-felix-and-hugo-white-of-the-maccabees-lhjr6xgqt5f

Secker, J., Hacking, S., Spandler, H., Kent, L. and Shenton, J. (2007) *Mental Health, Social Inclusion and Arts: Developing the Evidence Base.* Chelmsford: The Anglia Ruskin/UCLan Research Team. Accessed on 10/10/2017 at http://clok.uclan.ac.uk/3846/1/Arts.MH.FinalReportforweb.pdf

Seligman, M. (2011) *Flourish: A New Understanding of Happiness and Well-Being – and How to Achieve Them.* London: Nicholas Brealey Publishers.

Servan-Schreiber, D. (2011) *Not the Last Goodbye: Reflections on Life, Death, Healing and Cancer.* London: Pan Macmillan.

Sissay, L. (2014) *Superman was a Foundling.* London: The Foundling Museum. [Poem printed on the walls of the museum cafe.]

Silverman, P.R. (2000) *Never Too Young to Know: Death in Children's Lives.* New York: Oxford University Press.

Silverman, P.R. and Worden, J.W. (1992) 'Children's reactions in the early months after the death of a parent.' *The American Journal of Orthopsychiatry 62*, 1, 93–104.

Sjoqvist, S. (ed.) (2007) *Still Here with Me: Teenagers and Children on Losing a Parent.* London: Jessica Kingsley Publishers.

Smith, S. and. Pennells, Sister M. (eds) (1995) *Interventions with Bereaved Children.* London: Jessica Kingsley Publishers.

Sofka, C.J., Noppe Cupit, I. and Gilbert, K.R. (2012) *Dying, Death and Grief in an Online Universe.* New York: Springer.

Solomon, A. (2016) 'Literature about medicine may be the only thing that can save us.' *The Guardian*, 22 April, p.3.

Staricoff, R. (2004) Arts in Health: A Review of the Medical Literature. Arts Council England. Accessed on 2/8/2017 at www.artshealthandwellbeing. org.uk/resources/research/arts-in-health-review-medical-literature

Stokes, J. (2004) *Then, Now and Always: Supporting Children as They Journey through Grief: A Guide for Practitioners.* Cheltenham: Winston's Wish.

Stokes, J. (2009) 'Resilience and bereaved children. Helping a child to develop a resilient mind-set following the death of a parent.' *Bereavement Care 28*, 1, 9–16.

The Story Behind Luna's Red Hat (2015) [Blog] JKP Blog. Available at: www.jkp.com/ jkpblog/2015/05/the-story-behind-lunas-red-hat [Accessed 2/1/2018].

Stroebe, M. and Schut, H. (1999) 'The dual model of coping with bereavement: Rationale and description.' *Death Studies 23*, 197–224.

Stubbs, D., Ailovic, K., Stokes, J. and Howells, K. (2008) *Family assessment: Guidelines for child bereavement practitioners.* Cheltenham: Winston's Wish.

Stuckey, H.L. and Nobel, J. (2010) 'The connection between art, healing and public health: A review of current literature.' *American Journal of Public Health 100*, 2, February, 254–263.

Suzuki, Y. (2011) 'Our quest for meaning in the face of nature's wrath: Reflection on the Tohoku earthquake and tsunami.' *Bereavement Care 30*, 3, December, 2–4.

Tracey, A. (2011) 'Perpetual loss and pervasive grief: Daughters speak about the death of their mother in childhood.' *Bereavement Care* 30, 3, December, 17–24.

Trickey, D. (2005) 'Young people bereaved by suicide: What hinders and what helps.' *Bereavement Care 24*, 1, Spring, 11–14.

Turner, M. (2001) 'Tackling children's primitive fears during the grieving process.' *Bereavement Care 20*, 2, Summer, 22–25.

UNICEF (1992) *United Nations Convention on the Rights of the Child.* Accessed on 1/11/2017 at www.unicef.org.uk/what-we-do/un-convention-child-rights

Valentine, C. (2008) *Bereavement Narratives: Continuing Bonds in the 21st Century.* London: Routledge.

Valentine, C. (2009) 'Continuing bonds after bereavement: A cross cultural perspective.' *Bereavement Care 28*, 2, 6–11.

Varley, S. (2013) *Badger's Parting Gifts.* London: Andersen Press Ltd.

Vercoe, E. and Abramowski, K. (2004) *The Grief Book: Strategies for Young People.* Fitzroy, VIC: Black Dog Books.

Vickio, C.J. (1999) 'Together in spirit: Keeping our relationships alive when loved ones die.' *Death Studies 23*, 2, March, 161–175.

Walter, T. (1996) 'A new model of grief: Bereavement and biography.' *Mortality 1*, 1, 7–25.

Walter, T. (1999) *On Bereavement: The Culture of Grief.* Buckingham: Open University Press.

Walter, T. (2006) 'Telling the dead man's tale: Bridging the gap between the living and the dead.' *Bereavement Care 25*, 2, 23–26.

Walter, T. (2017) 'Promote, oppose, accommodate or compensate? Four ways religion can interact with society's death practices.' *Bereavement Care 36*, 1, 19–24.

Waskett, D.A. (1995) 'Chairing the Child: A Seat of Bereavement.' In S.C. Smith and Sister M. Pennells (eds) *Interventions with Bereaved Children* (pp.45–67). London: Jessica Kingsley Publishers.

Way, P. (2010) 'That isn't really how it works: Discussing questions of life, death and afterlife with bereaved children and young people.' *Bereavement Care 29*, 2, 17–20.

Westerink, D. and Stroebe, M. (2013) 'The death of a grandparent: Kaey's story.' *Bereavement Care 31*, 1, April, 6–10.

Wilkinson, F. (2017) 'I was 24 when my mother Sara died.' *Bereavement Care 36*, 2, 51–53.

Wilson, J., Gabriel, L. and James, H. (2016) 'Making sense of loss and grief: The value of in-depth assessments.' *Bereavement Care 35*, 2, 67–77.

Wilson, M. (2011) 'Exploring the efficacy of a bereavement support group for male category C prisoners: A pilot study.' *Bereavement Care 30*, 3, December, 10–16.

Winston's Wish (2013) *You Just Don't Understand: Supporting Bereaved Teenagers.* Cheltenham: Winston's Wish.

Worden, J.W. (1996) *Children and Grief: When a Parent Dies.* New York: The Guilford Press.

Yalom, I. (1980) *Existential Psychotherapy.* New York: Basic Books.

Yalom, I. (2011) *Staring at the Sun: Being at Peace with Your Own Mortality.* London: Piatkus.

Subject Index

Acorns Children's Hospice Trust 44–5, 53
acrostics 105
afterlife 76
'aftershocks' 17
ancestors 36–7
angels 69–70
anniversaries 16–18
anticipatory grief 96–103
  dreams as 63
aromatherapy 89
arts see creative approaches
Autistic Spectrum Disorder (ASD) 47
autobiographical art 57–8

bibliotherapy 111–12
books
  for 5- to 8-year-old 112–16
  for 9- to 12-year-old 117–20
  for 13- to 16-year-old 120–3
bunting of memories 60

Child Bereavement Network (CBN) 18, 42, 78

childhood bereavement 7–8
Childhood Bereavement UK (CBUK) 7, 16–17, 33, 43, 86
clay landscape of loss 60
closure 16
collage work 58
communication/conversations 39–40
  dreams as 62–4
  end-of-life 93–5, 96, 97, 99, 101–3
  final 103
  funerals 45–8
  importance of 40–2, 96
  sibling death 42–5
  see also online memorials
competence and wellbeing 88–9
complicated grief 85
continuing bonds, value of 12–16
creative approaches 51–60, 100–1, 109
  dreams 66
  cultural traditions 13–14
  ancestors 36–7
  worry dolls 58–9
  see also spirituality

digital legacy 51
dignity therapy 106–7
dreams and nightmares 61–2
  as anticipatory grief 63
  following bereavement 62–4
  spiritual dimension 68–71, 75
  themes 64–5
  and traumatic death 65–7
  visitation 67–8
dual model of coping with loss 12

'eminent orphans' 35
emotional self-care 84, 88
empathy 106
end-of-life care 93–5
  anticipatory grief 96–103
  importance of empathy 106
  letter writing 108
  list-making 108–9
  living with dying 107
  narrative medicine 103–6
expressive writing 52–4

family systems
  open 40–1
  sibling death 45
fear
  of death 31
  of losing other parent
    56–7, 63, 64–5
  and physical response
    to grief 82
  and sibling death 42–3
Foundling Museum,
  London 23
funerals 45–8

glass beads memory vase
  59–60
God/Allah 69, 70, 71
gratitude 86–7
grieving process 8–9,
  11–13
growth
  following sibling death
    45
  post-traumatic growth
    (PTG) 34, 55

Heads Together (charity)
  35–6
heaven 71
hero's journey 29–33
hope 86, 102–3
hospices 35–6, 44–5, 53,
  101, 105, 108
'Humpty Dumpty' 27

journal writing 25–6,
  32–3, 55–6

knitted squares: 'Love
  Wrap' 59

landscape of loss 60
learning disabilities/
  special educational
  needs 47, 73
legacies 37–8, 106
  digital 51
list-making 108
listening 41
loss-oriented behaviour
  12

love, receiving 80–2
'Love Wrap' 59

'magical thinking' 39–40,
  91–2
meaningful life 90
mementos 22–4
memorials 21–2
  online 48, 49–51
  see also creative
    approaches
memory boxes 24–5, 106
memory journals 25–6
mind mapping 56–7
mindfulness 87–8
music/songs 42, 68, 86,
  89, 107

narrative medicine
  103–6
narrative therapy 14–15
National Association
  for Loss and Grief
  (NALAG), Australia
  59
near death experience
  (NDE) 74–6
nightmares see dreams
  and nightmares

online forums and apps
  123–7
online memorials 48,
  49–51

palliative care see end-of-
  life care
paper boats 59
personal stories, sharing
  35–6
photographs 23, 24, 25,
  26, 36, 106
physical self-care 82–3
poetry 54
post-traumatic growth
  (PTG) 34, 55
pre-bereavement
  counselling 101
Princes William and
  Harry 35–6

religion see spirituality
resilience 18–21
restoration-oriented
  behaviour 12
rituals 103
rumination, avoiding 85

self-acceptance 84–5
self-care 9–10
  methods 80–92
  responses to
    bereavement 77–9
sensory comfort 89
shapeshifting dreams 65
sibling death 42–5
  anticipatory grief 98
  collage work 58
  expressive writing and
    poetry 53–4
  and spirituality 73
sleeping 86
  see also dreams and
    nightmares
social and emotional
  connections 85–6
social media 48, 49–51
social support 90–1
songs/music 42, 68, 86,
  89, 107
special days 16–18
special educational
  needs/learning
  disabilities 47, 73
spirituality 71–4
  and afterlife 76
  and dreams 68–71, 75
  and end-of-life care 98
  and meaningful life 90
  and near death
    experience (NDE)
    74–6
  and rituals 103
stories 27–9
  ancestors 36–7
  hero's journey 29–33
  as lasting legacies 37–8
  personal 35–6
  of unexpected gifts
    33–5
  see also narrative
    medicine; narrative
    therapy

stress-resistance *see* resilience
suicide 50, 66–7, 77, 86
survivor guilt 66, 99–100

thanablogging 49
thanatechnology 49
'tokens' 23
traumatic death 65–7, 72, 73, 77, 84
truthfulness 67, 93, 95, 96, 97–8, 99, 105–6

unexpected gifts 33–5
United Nations Convention on the Rights of the Child (UNCRC) 44

visitation dreams 67–8

web memorials 49–50
wellbeing and competence 88–9
worry dolls 58–9

writing
  activities 104–5
  expressive 52–4
  journals 25–6, 32–3, 55–6
  letters 108
  lists 108–9

Author Index

Abramowski, K. 67
Adams, K. 67, 68–9, 75
Albom, M. 82
All Party Parliamentary Group on Arts, Health and Wellbeing Inquiry 51
Almond, D. 28
Anderson, R. 15
Arens, G. 44, 45
Ariès, P. 80
Atwater, P.M.H. 75
Auster, P. 35

Bailey, L. 50
Baldwin, S.A. 61
Balk, D.E. 41, 72
Bank, S.P. 43
Barnes, J. 97
Barrett, D. 63
Barrie, J.M. 31–2
Basile, R. 63
Bassett, D.J. 50
Bastida, E. 62
Batten, M. 61, 73
Baum, L.F. 30
Becker, S.H. 32
Bell, J. 50
Bellous, J.E. 71
Berry, E. 54
Blackman, N. 73
Bosacki, S. 71
Brake 69
Brams-Prudeaux, J. 99
Brennan, F. 13

Brooks, R. 18
Brown, R. 52
Buchan, C. 100, 101
Bulkeley, K. 62, 67, 68
Bulkeley, P. 62, 68
Bull, A. 72
Bycock, I. 95
Bylund-Grenko, T. 96
Byrt, R. 52

Campanella, L. 54
Campbell, J. 29
Carey, J. 29
Carey, T. 106
Chan, C. 13
Child Bereavement Network (CBN) 18, 42, 78
Child Bereavement UK (CBUK) 7, 16–17, 33, 43, 86
Chochinov, H.M. 107
Chowns, G. 97, 105
Christ, G.H. 106
Co-Operative Funeral Care 48
Corr, C.A. 41
Coyle, N. 99
Cranwell, B. 46, 103
Crossley, D. 11

Darling, D. 75
Dash, M. 13
Davies, C. 35, 108
Dawson, P. 62

Demaria, T. 16, 34, 40, 47
Devita-Raeburn, E. 43
Di Cuacco, J.A. 22
Dickinson, E. 80, 109
Didion, J. 39, 91
Donnelly, J. 94
Dougy Center 99
Draper, A. 96
Duerden, N. 37
Dyregrov, A. 92–3

Emmons, R.A. 75

Fairfield, P. 93
Fenwick, E. 74, 75
Fenwick, P. 74, 75
Ferrell, B.R. 99
Ferris, L.R. 51
Fitzgerald, S. 53–4
Forward, D.R. 43
Foster, T.L. 13–14, 62–3
Fox, J. 41
Fuller, A. 80

Gabriel, L. 18
Gaines, A.G. 47
Garfield, P. 63
Garlie, N. 43
Gilbert, K. 49
Gillies, J. 61
Gladwell, M. 35
Glover, E. 52
Goldstein, S. 18
Golightly, A. 20

Gopnik, A. 14
Gordon, J. 25
Graves, D. 53
Gray, S. 55
Grimmitt, M. 69–70
Grosz, S. 28–9
Grove, J. 70

Hall, C.W. 42
Hardinge, F. 23
Harrison, R. 7
Hartman, E. 63
Hay, D. 71
Heaney, S. 54
Hedges, D. 102–3
Hedtke, L. 14
Higson, C. 30
Hirooka, K. 34
Horwitz, T. 37
Hoyle, E. 55
Huffington, A. 94
Hugo, V. 80
Hyde, B. 67, 75

Ishida, M. 62

Jacobs, W.J. 71
James, H. 18
Jeffers, O. 29
Jessop, J. 33–4
Joseph, S. 35
Jung, C.G. 69

Kabat-Zinn, J. 87–8
Kahn, M.D. 43
Kellaway, J. 102
Kennedy, D. 50
Klass, D. 36, 63, 74
Kleinman, A. 21
Knudson, R.M. 32
Koehler, K. 47
Krause, N. 62
Kübler-Ross, E. 70–1,
    91, 94
Kuhl, P.K. 14

Laity, P. 35
Lemon, M. 72, 84
Lewis, C.S. 52, 63, 82
Lindenfield, G. 108
Lipsky, D. 47
Lowry, L. 44

McArdle, S. 52
MacConville, U. 21
McCullough, M.E. 75
Macpherson, C. 102
Maddrell, A. 49
Mallon, B. 8, 62, 65,
    67–8, 73, 99
Mantel, H. 46
Martin, A.M. 24
Maslow, A. 27
Meltzoff, A.N. 14
Mistiaen, V. 54
Mitchell, J. 58
Monroe, B. 9
Moore, K. 101
Moorjani, A. 76
Morpurgo, M. 28
Moss, J. 55, 106

Neimeyer, R.A. 8, 52,
    55, 61
Ness, P. 95
Nobel, J. 109
Noppe Cupit, I. 49
Norris, J. 51
Nye, R. 71

Office for National
    Statistics (ONS) 7
Oliviere, D. 9
Oltjenbruns, K.A. 61, 73

Packman, W. 43, 45
Parkes, C.M. 7, 104
Pascoe, J. 73
Pennebaker, J.W. 32, 52
Pennells, Sister M.
    11–12, 52, 98
Petrone, M.A. 51, 100–1
Pollack, W.S. 19
Polsky, M.E. 47
Porter, M. 40
Proust, M. 79

Ribbens McCarthy, J.
    33–4, 41
Riches, G. 62
Roberts, P. 49–50
Rosen, H. 43
Round, S. 29
Rowling, J.K. 30

Sacks, O. 104
Samuel, J. 40–1, 57, 79,
    98, 100, 102
Saner, E. 31, 86
Sartori, P. 76
Schonfeld, D.J. 16, 34,
    40, 47
Schut, H. 12, 52
Scott, D. 107
Secker, J. 51
Seligman, M. 88
Servan-Schreiber, D.
    37–8, 74, 76, 81, 88,
    99
Silverman, P.R. 12–13
Sissay, L. 23
Sjoqvist, S. 36
Smith, S. 11–12, 52, 98
Sofka, C.J. 49
Solomon, A. 103
Spencer, L. 70
Staricoff, R. 52, 60
Stokes, J. 15, 18, 19
Stroebe, M. 12, 42, 52, 91
Stubbs, D. 19
Stuckey, H.L. 109
Suzuki, Y. 41

Tracey, A. 41
Trickey, D. 67
Turner, M. 29

UNICEF 44

Valentine, C. 14, 34,
    58, 79
Varley, S. 15–16
Vercoe, E. 67
Vickio, C.J. 13

Walter, T. 21, 29, 36, 50
Waskett, D.A. 71
Way, P. 74
Westerink, D. 42, 91
White, M. 14
Wilson, J. 18
Wooley, R. 67
Worden, J.W. 12, 13, 62

Yalom, I. 31, 95